Friendly Intruders

Friendly Intruders

Childcare Professionals and Family Life

by Carole E. Joffe

UNIVERSITY OF CALIFORNIA PRESS
Berkeley • Los Angeles • London

University of California Press
Berkeley and Los Angeles, California
University of California Press, Ltd.
London, England
Copyright © 1977 by
The Regents of the University of California
ISBN 0-520-02925-9
Library of Congress Catalog Card Number: 74-27289
Printed in the United States of America

For Fred

Contents

Preface

In 1971 Congress passed a Comprehensive Child Development Bill that authorized some two billion dollars for childcare services. The bill was vetoed by then-President Nixon, with an accompanying veto message that has since come to be regarded as one of the more remarkable documents of American social policy. The message read, in part:

> . . . our response to this challenge [child development] must . . . be consciously designed to cement the family in its rightful position as the keystone of our civilization. . . . Good public policy requires that we enhance rather than diminish both parental authority and parental involvement with children. . . .
>
> . . . for the Federal government to plunge headlong financially into supporting child development would commit the vast moral authority of the National Government to the side of communal approaches to childrearing over against the family-centered approach.
>
> This President, this government, is unwilling to take that step.[1]

In the period since 1971, these political objections to federal support of childcare have been overshadowed by economic ones. The problems of inflation and recession, and the resulting cutbacks in social services, have temporarily blunted the hopes of childcare advocates for new federal legislation. Childcare activity in the first half of the 1970s might best be characterized as a holding action; much of the effort of childcare forces has been directed toward protecting existing programs from Administration attempts at retrenchment.

Nevertheless, the conditions that prompted the 1971 bill are still very much with us. The number of families headed by women with children continues to rise dramatically; over the past decade such families may have increased at almost ten times the rate of two-parent families.[2] The

---

1. Richard Nixon, "Veto Message—Economic Opportunity Amendments of 1971."
2. Heather L. Ross and Isabel V. Sawhill, *Time of Transition: The Growth of Families Headed by Women,* pp. 1-2.

ix

eagerness of both single and married mothers of young children to work outside the home has not diminished; mothers of preschool and school-age children are acknowledged to account for much of the recent growth in female labor-force participation.[3] And the number of existing child-care facilities continues to be grossly inadequate; it is estimated that for the six million children under the age of six with working mothers, there are only one million licensed daycare places.[4]

These circumstances, combined with the continued spread of political consciousness among women, have kept the childcare issue alive—if not terribly well—in an area of austerity. It is reasonable to assume that an increased federal role in childcare is still on the national agenda. But the problems raised by governmental involvement in childcare go beyond the issue of economic feasibility.[5] The Nixon veto message reflects the political dynamite inherent in any attempt to construct a national childcare "policy"; and recent efforts to secure childcare legislation, in spite of their obviously dim prospects, have been met by an unusually vitriolic and anonymous smear campaign.[6] But for those involved in the childcare movement, the most important issue at this time is one of internal politics: who shall control the delivery of childcare? If federal funds for new preschool programs were made

3. A. H. Raskin, "The Changing Face of the Labor Force," *New York Times,* February 15, 1976, p. 4; and Elizabeth Waldman, "Children of Working Mothers, 1974." Waldman points out the rise in the number of children with working mothers despite the falling birthrate (p. 64): "Since 1970, the number of children whose mothers were in the labor force has risen by 1.2 million, while the number of all children in families has dropped by 2.2 million."

4. U.S. Senate, Committee on Finance, *Child Care Data and Materials,* pp. 58-59. This figure refers to slots in daycare centers and family daycare homes. It does not include other arrangements for preschool children that are defined as "educational" and are typically half-day programs, such as kindergartens, nurseries, and Headstart programs. Latest figures available on enrollment in these "educational" programs show a participation of 76.1 percent of all five-year-olds in the U.S., 33.5 percent of four-year-olds, and 15.5 percent of three-year-olds. Linda Barker, "Preprimary Enrollment: October 1972," p. 3.

5. Estimates of the cost of providing additional childcare slots are provided by Abt Associates, *A Study in Child Care,* Vol. III: *Cost and Quality Issues for Operators,* Day Care and Child Development Council of America, "Standards and Costs for Day Care;" Mary Potter Rowe and Ralph D. Husby, "Economics of Child Care: Cost, Needs, and Issues;" U.S. Senate, Committee on Finance, *Child Care Data and Materials;* and Dennis R. Young and Richard R. Nelson, *Public Policy for Day Care of Young Children.*

6. Congressman Thomas P. O'Neil, "The Vicious and Dishonest Campaign against the Child and Family Services Bill," *Congressional Record,* Vol. 121, n. 175, December 1, 1975, H11552-H11559.

available tomorrow, under whose auspices would such programs be offered? The major struggle is between the American Federation of Teachers and its allies and a coalition of other professional and community groups. The AFT argues that exclusive control of new programs should be given to the public schools; opponents want to preserve and promote more diversified sponsorship.

I hope that this book will contribute to informed debate on childcare policy. By offering a close look at one example of educationally defined childcare delivered through public schools, it may help in evaluating the claims of opposing factions within the childcare movement. I hope that it will also provide a concrete basis for approaching two larger, more fundamental questions raised by childcare: the professionalization of childcare services, and the relationship of childcare systems to family life.

Acknowledgments

The cooperation I received from staff members and parent-clients of the early childhood programs in the Berkeley public schools made possible the study reported in this book. I am most grateful to the supervisors, teachers, and parents who allowed me such an intimate view of their negotiations with one another. While it is perhaps inevitable that a sociological analysis of any institution demands a certain skepticism, I trust that the following pages will also convey the respect I have for the collective endeavors I saw. Most of my informants must remain anonymous, but I would like to acknowledge the special contribution of Mildred Messinger, of the Berkeley Unified School District. Her observations added much to my understanding of early childhood education, and her companionship made the process of this study even more pleasant.

This study was originally written as a thesis at the University of California, Berkeley, and I would like once again to thank the members of my committee: Robert Blauner, Arlie Hochschild, and Sheldon Messinger. I am particularly indebted to Sheldon Messinger for his invaluable guidance—both theoretical and practical—throughout the course of this project.

Joan Huber read critically an earlier draft and gave me excellent suggestions for revision. Others who gave me useful feedback include: Jessie Bernard, Patricia Bourne, Arlene Kaplan Daniels, Normal Denzin, Marvin Lazerson, Joan Mandle, Lillian Rubin, Charlotte Green Schwartz, Peggy Somers, Ann Swidler, and Joy Wood.

I would also like to thank Grant Barnes, Sheila Levine, and Gene Tanke for their editorial help; Barbara Levy Simon and James Hutchison for their research assistance, and The Graduate School of Social Work and Social Research of Bryn Mawr College for making their services possible; Zoe Bemis of the Canaday Library at Bryn Mawr College; and Lorraine Wright, who, with many other responsibilities to fulfill, expertly typed the final draft.

I am thankful to members of the Joffe family for their many expressions of encouragement. Finally, I am deeply grateful to my husband, Fred Block. His powers of critical thinking and enormous capacities for nurturance are both reflected in the pages that follow.

1

The Contradictions of Childcare

Perhaps the most interesting thing about childcare is the threat it poses to present understandings about family life. In a society which holds the nuclear family as its ideal, where the family is seen as the chief agency of childrearing, where mothers in particular are expected to assume chief responsibilities for preschool-aged children, then childcare—used here to refer to out-of-home care for young children for part of the day—may severely diminish the family's role. Parental authority may be weakened if very young children (those below the age of six) spend most of the day in the company of outsiders. Parental authority may be *especially* weakened if these outsiders have values significantly different from those of parents. Childcare—particularly if developed as a national "system," which is the logic of recent attempts at federal legislation—raises anew the agonizing and ultimately unanswerable question: To whom do young children really "belong"? To the parent or to society? At what point do children enter the realm of "public" life?

If we think about childcare in this way, then we can link our discussion to many other issues which revolve around ambiguities of responsibility, authority, and legal jurisdiction in matters of family life.[1] The evolution of compulsory school attendance laws, emergent

1. On state intervention in family life, see Grace Abbott, *The Child and the State;* Sanford Katz, *When Parents Fail: The Law's Response to Family Breakdown;* and Joseph

policies on child abuse and family intervention, distinctions recently being drawn between "biological" and "psychological" parents, and the current debates about the rights of minors to obtain birth control and abortion without parental consent—all these reflect the state's unwillingness to let the family be the sole arbitrator of a child's fate. Yet the immense amount of uncertainty that still exists over the proper handling of these issues shows how difficult it is to manage the tension between the interests of the state and the interests of the family.

It would be pretentious to burden our discussion with such concepts as "the role of the state" and "in loco parentis" if childcare meant no more than a three-year-old going happily off to nursery school for a few hours a day. But we must deal with a more complicated reality, which includes proposals for mandatory daycare for children of welfare recipients, the licensing of all new parents, the diagnosis of "behavioral disorders" in preschool populations, required parental education in public high schools, and the enrollment of infants in school-affiliated programs.[2]

Thus, although the proponents of childcare (myself among them) most often state the "childcare problem" as one of an insufficient supply of programs, we must remember that for others, especially the unwilling recipients of mandated services, the problem is rather too many such programs—or any at all. To understand childcare fully, we must recognize its dualistic character: like other social services, it contains possibilities both for "liberation" and for social control.[3] In this chapter we shall examine some of these issues closely, from this dualistic perspective. First, we shall see that historically there has never been in this country anything approaching a coherent universal childcare "system" of the sort that exists in some other societies.[4] The failure to

---

Goldstein *et al.*, *Beyond the Best Interests of the Child.* The growing literature on "children's rights" is also very relevant in this connection. See especially Paul Adams *et al.*, *Children's Rights: Toward the Liberation of the Child; Harvard Educational Review,* special issue on "Children's Rights;" and Albert Wilkerson, *The Rights of Children: Emergent Concepts in Law and Society.*

2. For a general critique of the coercive possibilities of childcare, see Katherine Ellis and Rosalind Petchesky, "Children of the Corporate Dream: An Analysis of Day Care as a Political Issue under Capitalism." On daycare and welfare, see Gilbert Steiner, *The State of Welfare,* Chapter 2. On required parental education, see Burton White, "Reassessing our Educational Priorities."

3. For a similar analysis of social services as simultaneously "too little" and "too much," see Barbara and John Ehrenreich, "Health Care and Social Control."

4. For a description of foreign childcare systems, see "A Look Abroad," in *Child Care—Who Cares?: Foreign and Domestic Infant and Early Childhood Development*

develop one is not only a reflection of the low priority given to children's needs on the national agenda—a charge that is consistently made by children's advocates.[5] It also indicates, I will argue, a deep cultural ambivalence about the very idea of childcare—an ambivalence especially about tampering with the functioning of "normal" families. The recent reemergence of a women's movement, with its own complex messages about the proper roles of women in both private and public life, has only heightened this ambivalence.

Although we may hesitate to tamper with some families, it is clearly wrong *not* to intervene in others. Public policies of "daycare," "early intervention," "compensatory education," and so forth have all been constructed for the children of parents who have been designated in some way "unfit" or poor. Thus we come to one of the most contradictory elements of the entire childcare debate: if we think of "childcare" as simply some form of group-care situation, with an "instructional" component, then there are actually *more* middle-and upper-income children in childcare than lower-income ones.[6] Yet the almost exclusive use of public funds for children of the poor or "unfit" (except in public school programs), and the close ties of such programs with social welfare, has brought to childcare a lingering cultural identity as a *stigmatized* service. These two related themes—the highly stratified nature of most childcare programs and the differing kinds of impact childcare seeks to make on its different clienteles—will be highlighted in the following brief historical survey of childcare arrangements in the United States.

HISTORICAL IMPLICATIONS

Only to a very limited extent has the development of childcare programs in the U.S. been acknowledged as a legitimate concern of government. The Mothers' Pension program, one of this country's

---

Policies, ed. Roby, pp. 299-432; and Uri Brofenbrenner, *Two Worlds of Childhood: The U.S. and U.S.S.R.*

5. Alvin Schorr, *Children and Decent People;* Patricia Bourne, *The Unconglomerated Agglomerate: Child Care and the Public Sector.*

6. This calculation includes public and private kindergartens. It does not include daycare centers. Middle and upper-middle-income children are enrolled disproportionately in kindergarten and private nursery schools. Lower-income children are disproportionately represented at the pre-kindergarten level in publicly controlled, all-day programs. See Linda Barker, "Preprimary Enrollment: October 1972." See also footnote 10, Chapter Five, this book.

earliest social policy measures, is far more revealing of governmental attitudes toward changes in family structure, especially the entrance of women into the labor force. This program, which had its origins in the White House Conference on the Care of Dependent and Neglected Children in 1909, established grants to enable widows and wives of disabled men to stay home and care for their children. The basic principles of the Mothers' Pension movement, as summarized in a 1914 report of a Commission on Relief were these: the mother is the best guardian of her children; no woman in normal circumstances can be both breadwinner and homemaker for her family; and normal family life is the foundation of the State, and its conservation is an inherent duty of government.[7] The growth of this policy diminished the legitmacy of the major childcare institution of the period, the day nursery. The consensus that developed around Mothers' Pensions suggests that the combination of working mothers and institutional childcare was not seen as a preferred option for the "respectable poor."

There have been in this country, however, two very brief periods when there was a national childcare "policy"—and both, significantly enough, occurred during times of national emergency. During the Great Depression, the Works Progress Administration (WPA) established a network of more than 1700 nursery schools, which served about 75,000 children.[8] And during World War II, the Lanham Act made funding available for childcare centers; although figures vary, by the war's end, as many as one and a half million children may have attended childcare programs made possible by the Lanham Act.[9] For our purposes, what is most striking about these efforts is that neither affirmed the idea of childcare for its own sake. The primary objective of the WPA nurseries was to provide jobs for unemployed adults. The impetus behind the World War II centers was to enable women to work in war industries.

7. Robert Bremer, *Children and Youth in America: A Documentary History,* pp. 355-379. On the Mothers' Pension movement, see also Mark Leff, "Consensus for Reform: The Mothers' Pension Movement in the Progressive Era;" and Abbott, *The Child and the State,* pp. 229-247.

8. On WPA nurseries, see *Emergency Nursery Schools during the First Year (1933-34)* and *Emergency Nursery Schools during the Second Year (1934-35);* Virginia Kerr, "One Step Forward—Two Steps Back: Child Care's Long American History;" and Samuel Braun and Esther P. Edwards, *History and Theory of Early Childhood Education.*

9. On World War II childcare, see Howard Dratch, "The Politics of Child Care in the 1940s;" Kerr, "One Step Forward—Two Steps Back;" Braun and Edwards, *The History and Theory of Early Childhood Education;* and J. E. Trey, "Women in the War Economy."

Accordingly after the war the Lanham Act centers were abruptly closed down in all but a few localities.

Although there has never been a permanent centrally coordinated national childcare "system," or even societal acknowledgment of the benefits of childcare, there has nevertheless been a great deal of "childcare" activity. We shall next survey briefly the origins of the dominant forms of of organized childcare—the day nursery or daycare center, the kindergarten, the nursery school, and the Head Start or compensatory education model—and then ask what light these forms shed on current policy dilemmas. The reader should bear in mind that alongside these four models there have always existed a wide range of other, less-formalized services, including the most common of all —leaving one's child with kin or neighbors.

Day Nursery Or Daycare Centers

Day nurseries started in this country in the mid-nineteenth century and were modeled on the earlier French *creches,* nurseries that were established near factories to aid working women.[10] In the U.S. many children spent the day unsupervised because of the considerable participation of immigrant women in the labor force. At the peak of the movement, in the first decade of the twentieth century, there were about 450 day nurseries in operation across the country, most of them founded by wealthy women in urban areas. The day nurseries, though started in most cases as independent efforts, gradually became closely connected to organized philanthropy: first to charity organizations and later to social work. There was considerable resistance to the idea of group care for young children, because of the feared disruption to family life; and nursery proponents in those days argued that the opposite was true—by providing an alternative to the institutionalization of unsupervised children, the nurseries were actually preserving the family.

The content of the earliest day nurseries was, in today's terms, largely "custodial." Their prime purpose was to provide a safe and healthful environment for children out of the care of their mothers. Proper nutrition, and above all, hygiene, appear to have been central concerns; for example, one recommendation of the 1905 Conference on Day Nurseries was that each nursery provide separate toothbrushes for each child and encourage brushing at least once a day. With the

10. The most useful secondary source available on the early day nurseries is Margaret Steinfels, *Who's Minding the Children? The History and Politics of Day Care in America.* Much of the following discussion draws on her account.

emergence in the late nineteenth century of an academic specialty in "early education," the day nurseries began to hire these newly trained personnel—first as kindergarten and then as nursery school teachers—in order to add an educational component to their programs.

Many of these early day nurseries routinely provided a range of services that are regarded as "experimental" in childcare circles today. Infants and sick children were accepted into the programs. In addition to regular all-day care (early morning to early evening), many of the nurseries also stood ready to provide weekend care if needed, after-school care for older children, and emergency night care. However, the incorporation of "professionals" into the day nursery staff created pressures to limit this very flexible set of services. Nursery school teachers apparently found the long hours of the day nursery program tiring; furthermore, in many cases they were unwilling to work with infants and toddlers, and argued that the youngest children should no longer be enrolled.[11]

Both the character and clientele of the day nurseries changed in important ways in the period after World War I. From institutions serving "respectably" poor families, in which the mother was circumstantially forced to work, the day nurseries increasingly became identified with a "pathological" population. There were several reasons for this. One was the drop in immigration in the postwar period. Another was the growing impact of the Mother's Pension policies; many working mothers now were encouraged to return home. A third factor was the professional development of social work, and the increasingly dominant position of social workers within the day nurseries. The clientele of the nurseries shifted largely to illegitimate children (whose mothers were ineligible for pensions); the purpose of the nurseries, now called "daycare centers," was to provide newly developing "casework" services for these pathological families. The simple fact of a woman's employment was no longer sufficient reason to merit enrollment in a daycare center. According to several observers, it was during this "casework" dominated phase that daycare became most strongly imprinted with the stigmatized identity it still carries today.[12]

In retrospect, one can see in daycare—particularly in its later phase—a dubious legacy for contemporary proponents of universal

11. See Ethel Beers, *Working Mothers and the Day Nursery;* and Steinfels, *Who's Minding the Children*, pp. 59-65, on the impact of "professionalism."

12. Steinfels, *Who's Minding the Children*, p. 63; Day Care Consultation Services, *Towards Comprehensive Child Care;* and Sheila Rothman, "Other People's Children."

childcare. Yet the very early day nurseries seem to represent a more ambiguous case. Albeit in very uneven and often contradictory ways, the day nurseries in some respects foreshadowed a model of a childcare institution that was responsive to the needs of the child *and* his or her family. This is reflected first in the flexibility of the hours of operation and in the ages at which children were permitted to be enrolled. In a more contradictory way, this responsiveness is shown in the fact that nurseries also served immigrant mothers with employment training and placement services. Yet, for the most part, the training was in "suitable" occupations such as domestic service and laundering. Mothers needing jobs were often placed in private homes as maids or put to work at the nurseries themselves. Contemporary critics further point out that the day nurseries were used by upper-class women as recruiting grounds for wet nurses.[13] However one chooses to evaluate the early-day nursery, there does appear to be one point of significant difference with the later daycare center, and the other developing forms of childcare: the legitimacy of women working outside the home was at least grudgingly acknowledged.

Kindergartens

Kindergartens, founded in Germany by the educator Friedrich Froebel, were brought to this country in the mid-nineteenth century by German immigrants.[14] The essential idea of the kindergarten was to create a special environment tailored to the particular needs of the child of preschool age: in a creative, yet orderly environment, the young child could overcome his self-centeredness and join in a society of his peers. The central activity of the kindergarten revolved around play with specially designed materials, Froebel's "gifts."

The first American kindergartens were privately run institutions for the children of the wealthy, but they soon spread to other sectors of the population and became an important component of social reform. Proponents began to conceive of kindergartens as unique instruments of Americanization for immigrant children and their parents. As one

13. Rothman, "Other People's Children."
14. On the early phase of the kindergarten movement in the United States, see Marvin Lazerson, *Origins of the Public School*, pp. 36-73, "The Historical Antecedents of Early Childhood Education," and "Social Reforms and Early Childhood Education: Some Historical Perspectives;" Robert Bremer, *Children and Youth in America*, pp. 1453-62; and Evelyn Weber, *The Kindergarten: Its Encounter with Educational Thought in America*.

enthusiastic administrator said, the kindergarten provides "our earliest opportunity to catch the little Russian, the little Italian, the little German, Pole, Syrian, and the rest and begin to make good American citizens of them."[15]

The kindergartens now began to move into settlement houses in immigrant neighborhoods. In some instances, trained kindergarten teachers were hired as staff members in day nurseries. It was during this settlement-house phase, according to some contemporary observers, that the kindergarten movement reached its finest hours: a vital part of the kindergarten program was interaction with the children's families, and home visits and parent activities at school became standard practices.

The success of kindergartens in working with immigrant children led to pressures for the institution to be absorbed into the public school system, a process which began in 1873. As Lazerson's work has skillfully shown, this transition into the public school setting brought with it a subversion of earlier kindergarten principles—home visits and constant interactions with parents, a classroom atmosphere of freedom and spontaneity, and an emphasis on creative play rather than academic instruction. All these became more difficult to sustain, and kindergarten activities began to resemble those of the upper levels of schooling whose buildings they now shared.[16]

In some respects, therefore, kindergartens and day nurseries were similar kinds of movements, at times even coexisting in the same buildings. Both responded to the problems of immigration and urbanization. From a contemporary standpoint, both reflected in their programs a mixture of "progressive" impulses, as well as clearly paternalistic ones. From our perspective, the kindergarten movement was uniquely important because it was the first to develop trained personnel specifically interested in educational work with "preschool" children.

The Nursery School

The interest in educationally defined services for preschool children continued to spread during the period immediately after World War I, with the emergence of nursery schools and the further professional development of a speciality of "early childhood education."[17] The

15. Quoted in Bremer, *Children and Youth in America,* p. 1459.

16. Lazerson, "Social Reform and Early Childhood Education." See also Bremer, *Children and Youth in America,* p. 1456.

17. As sources on the development of an independent nursery-school movement in the 1920s and its subsequent history in the following decades, I have relied on the following:

MacMillan sisters, in England, and Dr. Maria Montessorri, in Italy, were the dominant influences on the first generation of American nursery educators. Each of these pioneering European efforts took place among slum children and was closely tied to efforts at social reform. Some of the earliest American nursery school teachers, many of whom had studied in Europe, took jobs in day nurseries or in settlement houses. Some started their own nursery schools in slum areas; the Ruggles Street School, founded by Abigail Eliot in Boston, was one of the most famous of these. But as the nursery school movement began to develop in the 1920s, there was less activity within "daycare," or among the poor in general, and the nursery school became quite firmly identified with a middle-class clientele. (In part, this decreased activity within daycare centers was a reflection of the growing dominance of social workers in these institutions.) Some nursery schools became affiliated with private progressive schools of the period, such as the Walden School and the Banks Street School in New York. Universities were also an important base for nursery schools in the 1920s: on many campuses, "lab schools" were established for student observation, teacher training, and child development research. In 1925 leaders of this new profession met to form a professional association, the National Committee on Nursery Schools.

Another type of nursery, in addition to the private and university-affiliated school, was the parent cooperative—a nursery, founded, and partially staffed, by parents themselves. The first recorded parent cooperative was founded in 1915 by a group of faculty wives at the University of Chicago; its purpose was to "offer an opportunity for wholesome play for the children, to give the mothers certain hours of leisure from child care, and to try the social venture of cooperation of mothers in childcare."[18] Parent cooperatives spread quickly, and by 1930 there were about 260 of them.[19]

Although most nursery teachers of the 1920s were trained as "educators," they did not consider themselves part of the mainstream

---

Michael Auleta, *Foundations of Early Childhood Education: Readings;* Braun and Edwards, *History and Theory of Early Childhood Education;* Edith Dowley, "Perspectives on Early Childhood Education;" Abigail Eliot, "Nursery Schools Fifty Years Ago;" Lazerson, "Historical Antecedents of Early Childhood Education;" and National Society for the Study of Education, *Preschool and Parental Education.*

18. National Society for the Study of Education, *Preschool and Parental Education,* p. 29.

19. Mary Dabney Davis and Rowena Hansen, *Nursery Schools: Their Development and Current Practices in the United States.*

of public education. Their strongest ties, philosophically and organizationally, were to the progressive educational movement, which was reaching the height of its prominence in the 1920s. The curriculum of the typical nursery school in that period was thus a combination of the principles of Freud and Dewey: a high priority was placed on the emotional well-being of children and their rate of social maturation. The most characteristic activity in the nursery, as in the earlier kindergarten, was play. Omwake suggests to us the importance of a "play" orientation in the training of nursery educators of the 1920s: "In the early days of the nursery school movement, such phrases as good play environment, appropriate play experiences, free play, dramatic play, group play, parallel and solitary play, quiet play, play materials comprised much of the teacher's professional vocabulary."[20]

Nursery teachers of this period made a deliberate effort to avoid "academic" instruction. The many controversies over the teaching of reading typified their attitudes toward basic skill instruction. In response to criticism for not teaching reading, nursery educators responded that young children were not psychologically or physically "ready" to read—in part because their eye muscles were insufficiently developed—and that a far more profitable strategy was to develop "reading readiness" by providing experiences which would "predispose the young toward books."[21]

The professional development of early childhood education was given a further boost by the creation of WPA nurseries during the Depression. This occurred suddenly, and was not immediately welcomed by the recently founded National Committee on Nursery Schools, which feared a drop in the standards for early childhood programs. The committee demanded—and received—a supervisory role

---

20. Evelyn Omwake, "The Child's Estate," p. 285.

21. Lazerson, "The Historical Antecedents of Early Childhood Education," pp. 49-50. The early nursery movement's firm opposition to "academic" instruction was summed up as follows by Grace Owen, an influential British educator: "No mention has been made of instruction in the Nursery School because in any formal sense it has no place. No reading, no writing, no number lessons should on any account be required—no object lessons as commonly known should be allowed, for the time for these things has not yet come. Up to the age of six, the child is usually fully occupied in mind and body with learning from actual experience: he is busily taking in ideas from the world about him, he is gaining information by means of his own questionings of grown-up people—he is experimenting with his limbs, his senses, his hands, in a thousand ways." (Grace Owen, *Nursery School Education*, p. 25.) For similar statements of early nursery philosophy, see Josephine Foster and Marion L. Mattson, *Nursery School Education;* Emma Henton,

in the administration of the project. The corps of experienced nursery personnel increased dramatically: of the 3775 teachers involved in the WPA programs at the end of the second year, some 2000 had been teachers, but only 158 had had previous nursery experience.[22]

The Lanham Act centers of World War II also furthered the aims of early childhood educators, though in a more indirect way. There was much interprofessional and interagency rivalry over the delivery of Lanham Act funds: in particular, there emerged a deep rivalry between early childhood educators and social workers over the proper character of the new facilities. Social workers urged that the funds be used for family (home-based) daycare and casework, whereas the early educators argued for group care. There were never any clear legal or administrative guidelines about how Lanham Act funds were to be destributed, but inasmuch as many of the funds were given to local school districts, the nursery forces won a partial victory. Once again, if only briefly, the government was supporting educationally defined services for preschool children.

In assessing the nursery school's place in the historical development of childcare services, two facts are of central importance. First, except for the short-lived WPA and Lanham Act experiments during the Depression and World War II, the nursery schools were always "child-centered"—that is, their primary purpose was defined as the enrichment of the child. With their half-day programs, sometimes offered only three days a week, and with some programs calling for parent participation, they were never designed as a mechanism to allow mothers to work. Second, their almost exclusive association with a middle-class, often academic, clientele—and their lack of ties with welfare agencies—kept the nursery schools free of the social stigma that was associated with daycare.

Head Start And Compensatory Education

The Head Start program was established in 1965 as part of the War on Poverty. It has proved to be one of the most enduring of the "Great Society" programs of the Johnson administration; it survived the dismantling of the Office of Economic Opportunity and is administratively located in the Department of Health, Education, and Welfare

---

"The Nursery School Movement in England and America;" Harriet M. Johnson, *Children in the Nursery School;* and Catherine Landreth, *Education of the Young Child.*

22. *Emergency Nursery Schools during the Second Year (1934-35).*

(H.E.W.). In 1975, Head Start was serving some 350,000 children yearly.

Head Start, and the similar compensatory education projects it spawned, was very much a part of the social reform efforts of the times. The stated mission of Head Start was to overcome, by early intervention, the deficiencies of "culturally deprived" children and prepare them for entrance into primary school. This "head start" was to be achieved through a combination of medical, psychological, nutritional, and educational services. Although there were considerable variations among different Head Start programs, in many cases the close link to the children's forthcoming school careers meant a heavy emphasis on cognitive instruction.

One immediate consequence of Head Start was a rejuvenation of the field of child development. The Head Start era inspired a staggering amount of research on young children, especially those labeled "disadvantaged."[23] The learning possibilities of preschool children came under new scrutiny: influential articles by leading scholars generated much excitement—both within the field and without—about the awesome intellectual tasks of the first five years of life.[24] Similarly, there occurred in child development circles a strong revival of interest in earlier theoreticians such as Piaget and Vygotsky.

Notwithstanding its staying power and the close ties of top Head Start officials to the child development establishment, Head Start has been controversial since its inception. Perhaps the most important question has been, How much do children really benefit from the program? A large government-sponsored survey of Head Start in 1969 claimed that the effects of the program on its graduates were negligible.[25] This evaluation itself generated a tremendous conflict, not only over the reliability of the data, but over the appropriateness of measuring Head Start achievements in terms of such indicators as I.Q. gains. To date, there is little consensus on how effective Head Start has been—or, indeed, on what criteria its "effectiveness" should be measured.

---

23. A useful bibliographic guide to this huge literature is Philip Lichtenberg and Dolores Norton, *Cognitive and Mental Development in the First Five Years.*

24. Among the key works in this genre are Benjamin Bloom, *Stability and Change in Human Characteristics;* J. McVicker Hunt, *Human Intelligence;* Jerome Bruner, "The Course of Cognitive Growth;" and, most recently, Burton White, *The First Three Years of Life.*

25. Westinghouse Learning Corporation, *The Impact of Project Head Start: An Evaluation of the Effects of Head Start on Children's Cognitive and Affective Development.*

Another running controversy concerns the proper relationship between Head Start programs and the "community," especially the parents of Head Start children. Emerging as it did from the War on Poverty, Head Start was promoted with much rhetoric about "community participation." Nearly all Head Start programs have parents and "community persons" on their boards and at various staff levels. In some cases, however, like that of the Child Development Group of Mississippi, Head Start's very success in generating close ties with the "community" became a political fiasco.[26] In the Mississippi case, Head Start was accused of serving as a base of operations for civil rights activists, and its right to funding was challenged. On the other hand, various other Head Start programs have been periodically accused by their clients of being insufficiently responsive to community needs. However, it is generally acknowledged that Head Start has been successful in serving as a career base for parents; it was recently estimated that some 10,000 Head Start parents have used the programs as stepping-stones to gaining teacher credentials.[27]

Another problematic aspect of the relationship between Head Start and parents lies in the program's original ideological base of "cultural deprivation." Like the wider compensatory education movement of which it is a part, Head Start faces a continuing struggle to develop theories of why children fail and policies of intervention that are not offensive to its (largely minority) constituency.[28] "Home Start," one of Head Start's latest offshoots, in which parents are visited in their homes and given instruction on childrearing, carries this ambiguity one step further.[29]

Comparing Head Start with the other three earlier childcare models, we can immediately see a basic continuity. Head Start maintains the tradition of highly stratified childcare, with its programs being limited

26. For a participant's detailed account of the CDGM controversy, see Polly Greenberg, *The Devil Has Slippery Shoes.*

27. *New York Times,* June 8, 1975.

28. For a critique of Head Start and similar compensatory programs, see Stephen and Joan Baratz, "Early Childhood Intervention: The Social Science Base of Institutional Racism."

29. On Home Start, see Christopher Barbrack and Delia Horton, "Educational Intervention in the Home and Paraprofessional Career Development: A First Generation Mother Study;" Barbrack, "Educational Intervention in the Home and Paraprofessional Career Development: A Second Generation Mother Study with Emphasis on Costs and Benefits;" and Susan Gray, "Home Visiting Programs for Parents of Young Children." For a black comment on Home Start, see Evelyn Moore, "It's Happening . . . in Childcare."

to a low-income population. Another similarity with the very early day nursery, but one which has developed to a much higher degree in Head Start, is the notion that the childcare facility itself becomes a career base for some parents.

Although Head Start continued the pattern of stratified services, it broke with tradition over the issue of what services the poor would get. Until Head Start, a basic division existed between the largely custodial care offered to poor children in daycare, and the "enrichment" programs which were offered mostly to the middle-class clientele of nursery schools. Head Start meant that the poor would now receive a full battery of "comprehensive" childcare services, including an educational component.

The association of Head Start with educationally defined services has had tremendous implications for the professional development of early childhood education. It brought a huge new clientele and program base to a profession that was formerly restricted to serving the middle class in mostly private nursery schools, and it stimulated an enormous amount of research activity in child development. Largely in response to the Head Start phenomenon, moreover, a new technology of early learning materials was created: talking typewriters, dozens of "educational games," parent-child toy libraries, and other new materials were developed to meet the demands of a vastly expanded early childhood market.[30]

Yet Head Start and similar preschool compensatory efforts also led to a crisis within established early childhood education circles. The close link, in the minds of planners and clients alike, between Head Start and the future success of children in school led in many instances to disciplined, often rigorous, forms of academic instruction. For many, the traditional nursery school goals of adjustment, control of aggression, and emotional well-being were no longer sufficient; similarly, the time-honored nursery-school emphasis on "creative play" was challenged. Early childhood educators are now split into two camps—the "old guard" nursery-school teachers and the new "cognitivists."[31] The

30. See especially Ann Cook and Herbert Mack, "Business in Education: The Discovery Center Hustle;" and Maya Pines, *Revolution in Learning.*

31. This split is discussed in Pines, *Revolution in Learning,* Chapter One. See, also, Helen Beck, "Pressure in the Nursery;" Annie Butler, "Early Childhood Education: A Perspective on Basics;" Dorothy Cohen, "This Day's Child in School;" Dorothy Gross, "Encouraging the Curious Mind: Through the Curriculum;" Elizabeth Hirsch, "Accountability: A Danger to Humanistic Education;" and John Sandberg and Joanne Pohlman, "Reading on the *Child's* Terms."

old guard is appalled by what it considers an overdemanding, "pressure-cooker" approach to learning and a betrayal of various essential components of nursery-school ideology, such as the developmental value of play. The new teachers see their accusers as hopelessly class-biased, as well as unforgiveably naive about the actual learning abilities of young children.

By its sheer size and political staying power Head Start more than any other program, has undoubtedly led millions to accept as normal the idea of group care for young children. A more ambiguous legacy of Head Start is the idea that the purveyors of preschool services can be held accountable for the success or failure of their efforts. The inflated expectations of Head Start's original planners and its continued status as a federally funded program have led to a public obsession with tangible "results" that has not been focused on other forms of childcare.

CURRENT DILEMMAS OF CHILDCARE POLICY

The history of childcare in the United States is thus a history of diverse programs, offered under different auspices, to different populations, for different reasons. Imbedded in each of these different forms is choice about what a national system of childcare ought to be. Let us examine these choices systematically.

The first question to be answered in making any choice concerns the overall purpose of a childcare system. Should childcare be designed primarily in response to the needs of adults or to the needs of children? If it is adult-oriented, there is another choice to be made. Should it be concerned rather strictly with workforce participation—as a service to parents already working, or as a mechanism for preparing them to enter the labor force, which is the rationale for the present WIN program?[32] Or should it be conceived more broadly as a means of temporarily relieving parents—whether working or not—of the sole responsibility of caring for their children? Of course, childcare may be beneficial for *both* parent and child, but then one has to ask whether the needs of one party can be served without neglecting the needs of the other. For example, all-day care might be the most convenient form for the working parent but not the most beneficial form for the very young child.

Closely related to the problem of "purpose" is a second issue. For whom should nationally supported childcare be made available? Only

32. On the WIN Program and childcare, see Steiner, *The State of Welfare.*

for families in which both parents work? For working families below a certain income level? For children of welfare recipients? For children from inadequate or "deprived" backgrounds? For all children, irrespective of family circumstances?

A similar question exists about the most reasonable age at which children should be eligible for childcare. Most current preschool programs are designed for the three-to five-year-old age group. But some experts now advocate the benefits of infant care—once a staple of the earliest day nurseries.[33] Others argue that "childcare services" should begin at conception, with prenatal counseling for parents on nutrition and other matters.

A third question concerns the appropriate form and content of childcare programs. Is institution-based group care, with large numbers of children on the premises, the most appropriate form for children, especially those below the age of three? Or, as family daycare advocates argue, should a national childcare system also support home-based programs of small groups of children?[34] Whether home-based or institution-based, what should childcare programs actually *do?* All childcare must, by definition, provide adequate custodial care; but should it attempt to do *more?* If so, what? There are several current alternatives: the casework services offered by social workers in daycare programs; the educationally defined services of the traditional nursery school, with its emphasis on socio-emotional development, or of the compensatory education program, with its more academic orientation; and finally, the "comprehensive" package of programs such as Head Start, which offer a combination of health and educational services.

Firmly entwined with these three questions is one of the thorniest of all childcare policy issues, the proper role of parents in childcare programming. Because of tremendous cultural hesitations about childcare—especially about its problematic relationship to "family life"—virtually all publicly funded programs, and many private ones as well, have a rhetorical commitment to "parental involvement." But

---

33. Bettye Caldwell, "Infant Day Care—The Outcast Gains Respectability;" Alice Hoenig, "Curriculum for Infants in Day Care;" and *Voice for Children,* special issue on "Infant Care," January-February 1976.

34. Of early childhood professionals, June Solnit Sale and Arthur Emlen have been among the strongest defenders of family daycare. See Emlen, "Slogans, Slots and Slander: The Myth of Day Care Need;" and Sale, "Family Day Care: One Alternative in the Delivery of Developmental Services in Early Childhood," and "Watch: Family Day Care Mothers Work Together To Improve Services."

there is little agreement as to what, in fact, "parental involvement" actually means.[35] It can mean parents sitting on governing boards, setting program policy and hiring staff. In many instances, however, it can mean parents serving on boards as token figures, making no decisions of consequence whatsoever. Parent involvement sometimes means the actual participation of parents in the children's program; the funding of some programs is made conditional on a certain volume of parent participation.

Sometimes "parent involvement" can be interpreted to mean that parents as well as children should receive services from childcare providers. Thus in some day nurseries, parents receive casework services; in many nursery schools and Head Start programs, there are attempts at "parent education," which is the most complex aspect of an already difficult issue. Inescapably, any attempt by childcare personnel to provide "parent education" carries with it the suggestion that parents are currently performing inadequately. In compensatory programs, such as Head Start, where "interventive" services are delivered to parents whose children have been designated as "deficient," the difficulties of reconciling "parent education" with parental self-esteem are magnified.

Finally there is the problem that currently dominates legislative debate on childcare policy—the administration and control of childcare services. Federally supported childcare has always been essentially a "non-system," with confused lines of authority between federal, state, and local agencies, and with overlapping jurisdictions between health, education, and welfare bureaucracies. Strong educational forces, led by A.F.T. President Albert Shanker, are arguing that the allocation of new federal funds be used to create a universally available childcare system, to be located within the public schools.[36] The debate is not simply a squabble between professional groups seeking control of childcare. It involves the more fundamental question, often raised in current

35. Donald Miller, "Governing Child-Care Centers: Basic Considerations," discusses the range of parental participation.

36. The AFT position is spelled out in a union publication, "Early Childhood Education: A National Program." See also Albert Shanker, "Early Childhood Education Is a Job for the Public Schools," *New York Times,* September 9, 1974, p. 11; and "Statement before the Senate Subcommittee on Special Education Programs on the Child and Family Services Act of 1975." The May 1975 issue of the *American Teacher,* including the magazine section, *Quest,* carries numerous articles relating to the AFT's interest in securing prime sponsorship of early childhood programs.

Washington discussions, of whether *any* professional group should be given exclusive control childcare. At present, most of the children of working parents who are placed in childcare receive non-professionalized service: more than half are cared for by kin or babysitters and many of the others are placed in licensed or unlicensed "family daycare homes."[37] Are so many of these children being cared for in non-professional settings simply because "better" childcare is not available or accessible, as the professionals claim? Or, as others maintain, is the less professionalized, home-based arrangement actually preferred by working parents, for a variety of reasons? If so, should not public policy help make these kinds of arrangements more widely available?

One way of approaching this issue is to ask another question: What are the ideal qualifications of the childcare provider? What does one have to "know" to provide proper childcare? Should the presence of at least some persons with specialized training in child development be a necessary staff requirement? Or is affection and respect for children sufficient—and in fact more important than credentials? Non-professional providers of care make several arguments which suggest that "professionalism" may be detrimental to children's interests. They argue that precise job descriptions, fixed schedules, and possible unionization (which raises the possibility of strikes) are incompatible with taking care of very young children. At a city-wide meeting of childcare providers in Berkeley, California, the president of a local family daycare operators' association defended non-professional childcare and implied why many working parents in particular would find it attractive: "We don't have fancy degrees, but if your child is not toilet-trained yet, we'll take him. . . . If he's sick and you have to go to work, we'll take him. . . . If you get held up at work and are going to get here a little late, that's O.K., we don't close the doors at 5. . . . We'll love your child in our own home."

Established childcare professionals are predictably upset by the

37. Seth Low and Pearl Spindler, *Child Care Arrangements of Working Mothers in the United States;* Florence Ruderman, *Child Care and Working Mothers: A Study of Arrangements Made for Daytime Care of Children.* In her survey of working women in seven communities, Ruderman found that the most frequent arrangement—73 percent —was some form of in-home care. Of those using out-of-home arrangements, 14 percent used "family daycare" (for example, someone else's home) and only 4 percent used a daycare center or nursery school (pp. 211-212). It is interesting, however, that the small minority that used center facilities were among the respondents who were most *satisfied* with their child-care arrangements (p. 290).

suggestion that publicly supported childcare be delivered without professional supervision. They recite the childcare horror stories—children being tied to beds and so forth—that have occurred in proprietary situations.[38] Their argument is that childcare will never develop its full potential, and never win public acceptance as a universal service, unless it is delivered under professional auspices, according to the standards and regulations that only professional control would bring.

THE "WEAKNESS" OF CHILDCARE PROFESSIONALS

This book is about the struggle of childcare professionals—in particular, early childhood educators—to define and control public childcare programs. The struggle involves more than rivalries with competing professions. It also raises the fundamental question of whether any professional group should control childcare services. The issues, as we have seen, are not new; they have been alive since teachers and social workers began to enter the early day nurseries. But the possibility that national childcare legislation could be enacted soon, placing considerable resources at someone's command, has brought a new urgency to the old uncertainty about the role of professions in childcare.

The theoretical approach to professions and "professionalization" used in this book draws heavily on the work of Everett Hughes and his students. The rewards of "professional" status and the corresponding efforts made by workers in different occupations to achieve such a status are central preoccupations of this approach. As Hughes has expressed it:

> The concept "profession" in our society is not so much a descriptive term as one of value and prestige. It happens over and over that the people who practice an occupation attempt to revise the conceptions which their various publics have of the occupation and the people in it. In so doing, they also attempt to revise their conception of themselves and their work. The model which these occupations set before themselves is that of the "profession": thus the term "profession" is a symbol for a desired conception of one's work and hence, of one's self. The movement to "professionalize" an occupation is thus collective mobility of some among the people in an occupation."[39]

38. One of the chief documents exposing the range and quality of existing daycare facilities is Mary Dublin Keyserling, *Windows on Day Care,* a national survey commissioned by the National Council of Jewish Women.

39. Everett C. Hughes, *The Sociological Eye,* pp. 339-340.

The objective of sociologists working in this tradition is not to decide whether certain occupations merit classification as "professions."[40] Instead, the focus is on the *processes* of professionalization; it makes no difference that some occupations will never become as fully "professionalized" as others, because the interest is in observing the activities of any occupation as it moves toward its desired status. Medicine, which Hughes referred to as the "queen of the professions," and law, are often held up as the models to which other occupations aspire.

According to this approach, there are several things that members of an "upwardly mobile" occupation typically do as they seek to upgrade themselves. They begin to point to a body of knowledge that serves as a "technical base" for professional expertise. They lengthen the period of required training, and formalize credentials. They seek affiliation with universities as training sites. They increase the hierarchical ranking of their own activities, relegating more routine tasks to subordinates. They add a research component to what was once only a practice-oriented field. They establish professional associations. But most important of all, they attempt to establish exclusive control over the particular service they offer; they seek to be the only ones legally empowered to deliver such services. In his brilliant study of the medical profession, Freidson describes such control as the essence of the enormous power of the medical establishment: in the realm of health, doctors have gained "exclusive control over the exercise of a particular skill and captured exclusive right of access to goods and services the layman is likely to feel he needs."[41]

But the notion of "control" in this approach to the study of professions goes beyond the legally guaranteed powers of monopoly. "License and mandate," a key concept for Hughes, refers both to the narrower aspects of licensing by the state and to broader social *understandings* about professional prerogatives. The phrase conveys an element of trust that has been granted to a professional body; the profession, ideally, is mandated to define the public interest in matters relating to its particular speciality. In this sense, professionals not only perform services but also dictate public policy.[42]

40. *Ibid.*, p. 340. "In my own studies I passed from the false question: 'Is this occupation a profession?' to the more fundamental one: 'What are the circumstances in which people in an occupation attempt to turn it into a profession, and themselves into professional people?' and 'What are the steps by which they attempt to bring about identification with their valued model?' "

41. Eliot Freidson, *Professional Dominance*, p. 117.

42. Hughes, *The Sociological Eye*, p. 376; p. 424.

The concept of "control" also extends to the professionals' own sense of autonomy. Drawing again from Freidson's work we find that it is fundamental to the self-image of the doctor—that most "powerful" of professionals—that he expects to be able to control his work setting, without lay interference. As Freidson has written:

> *Belief* in the extraordinary character of the work and of the performer sustains the worker's claim that he must be able to exercise his own complex, individual judgment independently of others, that is, he must be independent and autonomous. While members of *most* occupations seek to be free to control the level and direction of their work efforts, it is distinct to professionalism to assert that such freedom is a necessary precondition for the proper performance of work.[43]

But the professionals' ideology of autonomy is not always shared by the consumers of their services. Accordingly, one creative part of the work of Hughes and his associates has been to highlight a fundamental antagonism within the professional-client relationship.[44] Members of virtually all professional groups who deal with the public are faced with periodic challenges to their authority: clients who refuse to do the professional's bidding, or who demand services the professional is unwilling to perform. What distinguishes the more powerful professions from others is their greater ability to remain impervious to such challenges.[45]

If we place early childhood education into this theoretical context, we would have to characterize it as a marginal or "weak" profession. It does, of course, have some "professional" attributes: a long history of affiliation with universities for the training of personnel; a lively research tradition; an internal split between "theoreticians" and "practitioners" (with various levels of practictioners); and several nationally active professional associations.

What early childhood education clearly lacks as a profession is a distinctive "license and mandate"—in both the narrow and the broad senses mentioned earlier—to deliver childcare services. It must compete for acceptance with neighboring professions, such as social work, and with a range of non-professional providers—family daycare homes,

---

43. Freidson, *Professional Dominance,* p. 154.

44. Hughes, *The Sociological Eye,* pp. 300-301; 345-346; Howard Becker, "The Teacher in the Authority System of the Public School," and "The Culture of a Deviant Group: The Dance Musician;" and Eliot Freidson, *Patients' Views of Medical Care.*

45. Freidson, *Professional Dominance,* p. 118.

private "proprietary daycare centers," and the latest variation on private care, "franchised" day care.[46] Although licensing requirements for childcare facilities exist in most states, they are often very casually enforced, and they usually deal only with the physical features of the facility, not with the qualifications of staff or the content of programs. Because childcare services are currently delivered under a hodgepodge of different arrangements, with minimal government regulation, it has been virtually impossible for any one group, such as early educators, to gain anything approaching "exclusive control."

But a more fundamental reason why early childhood education lacks a clear-cut mandate lies in the contradictory nature of the very idea of "professionalized childcare." As we have seen, professionalized childcare is often resisted because it is feared as a threat to parental authority. Yet from another perspective, one might argue that childcare workers, including early educators, have trouble being taken seriously as "professionals" precisely because their work itself—caring for young children—is so familiar and ordinary. Wilensky points out that in order be successful in claiming special expertise, a profession must steer away from "a vocabulary that sounds too familiar to everyone."[47] The heart of the problem for childcare workers is that the care of normal preschoolers is *very* "familiar to everyone," and especially to their parent-clients. Thus for a "weak" profession, like early childhood education, the main struggle with clients is not, as in the powerful professions, to withstand unacceptable demands; rather it is to be acknowledged as "professional" in the first place—to make the status leap from "babysitter" to "educator."

The status problems of early childhood educators are, of course, compounded by the overwhelmingly female composition of the profession.[48] Especially at the level of the practitioner, early childhood education is in the classic bind of the female profession, as described by Bernard.[49] Because their work is taking place in an area that has always been considered women's responsibility, the cultural response is that

46. See Joseph Featherstone, "Kentucky Fried Children;" and the *Wall Street Journal*, "Growing Pains: Day Care Franchises, Beset with Problems, Find Allure Is Fading," November 27, 1972.

47. Wilensky, "The Professionalization of Everyone?" p. 149.

48. Separate figures are not available for early childhood educators. Of those classified by the Census as "pre-kindergarten and kindergarten teachers" in 1970. there were 125,884 females and 2,340 males. U.S. Bureau of the Census, "Summary of Social and Economic Characteristics of Pre-kindergarten and Kindergarten Teachers, 1970."

49. Jessie Bernard, *Women and the Public Interest*.

such work is being performed out of "love and duty." It is thus considered "unseemly" when such women workers demand the prerogatives of a professional status.

Although we have categorized early childhood education as a "weak" profession, it is also correct to see it as a profession "on the make." The mid-1970s seem to be a particularly fateful moment for its expectations of upward mobility. A constellation of recent events —most notably the steadily increasing number of working mothers with young children, the reemergence of a women's movement, and the nationwide impact of Head Start—is changing the social meaning of childcare, and with it the public view of childcare workers. More specifically, it is possible that the fortunes of workers in early childhood education are being significantly shaped by current developments within the public schools. A considerable drop in school enrollment, with a resulting layoff of many teachers and the availability of many empty classrooms,[50] has caused public schools to become newly interested in early childhood programs.

Finally, although this study is theoretically guided by an interest in the process of professionalization, it cannot ignore the fact that we are dealing quite explicitly with political issues. The current struggle for control over childcare involves more than the use of new resources that might be provided by national childcare legislation. Its outcome, for better or worse, will answer certain basic questions about the social construction of early childhood: What understandings should we have of young children's needs and capacities? When, and under what circumstances, should they enter public life? Who should be their caretakers?

50. As of this writing, the latest figure available on abandoned classrooms was 18,005 during the school year 1970-1971. U.S. Department of HEW, *Digest of Educational Statistics,* 1974, p. 52. Government projections of school enrollment are for a 10 percent decrease between 1973 and 1983 from kindergarten through grade twelve. U.S. Department of HEW, *Projections of Educational Statistics to 1983-84,* p. 8. In spring 1975, the AFT claimed that between 100,000 and 150,000 currently employed school teachers were threatened with layoffs as of fall 1975, *American Teacher,* April 1975, p. 3.

2
Childcare in the Schools:
A Case Study

The issue of control is the major political controversy in current debate over national childcare policy. The controversy in the mid-1970s specifically centers around the demands of the public schools to receive exclusive jurisdiction over new childcare services. What would happen if the schools were to become successful in this struggle? What would childcare delivered through the schools actually mean? What implications would this have for the content of childcare programs? How would such a development bear upon the arguments of childcare opponents who fear the "institutionalization" of very young children? What consequences would this type of arrangement have for the often ambiguous relationship between childcare professionals and parents? Finally, what would this development on a national scale mean for the professional aspirations of early childhood educators, whom I have characterized as members of a "weak" profession?

In order to suggest some of the possible answers to these questions, the following chapters will examine closely a specific situation in which childcare sponsored by the public schools has existed for several years: the Early Childhood Education unit of the Berkeley, California, Unified School District (BUSD), which I studied during 1971-1973.[1] In looking

1. Since this study was completed, ECE underwent an administrative reorganization. See the Postscript at the end of this book.

24

at school-administered childcare in Berkeley, we are observing a model which is rapidly gaining acceptance in California and may well foreshadow a major form of publicly funded childcare elsewhere.

THE SETTING: ECE

During the years 1971-1973 the Early Childhood Education (ECE) unit of the Berkeley Unified School District provided over half of all available childcare spaces in Berkeley.[2] It operated "Parent-nurseries," half-day programs for two, three, and four-year-olds which require some parent participation; "Children's Centers," all-day care for preschool-age children of low-income working or student parents; and "Extended Care" programs before and after regular school for the school-age children of working parents. The "Early Learning Center" model, the organization's newest innovation, combines all three programs and their populations at one site.

ECE was created as a department within the BUSD in 1965. Its immediate task was to coordinate the district's two already existing preschool programs—the Children's Centers, which had their origins in the WPA nurseries of the Depression, and the Parent-nurseries, which had been administered through the Berkeley Adult School. A third program to come under the new ECE administration shortly thereafter was the State Preschool Program (Assembly Bill 1331), a half-day nursery program for children of welfare recipients, which was established by the California legislature in 1966.

There seem to have been two reasons for the district's interest in rejuvenating its early childhood programs in the mid-1960s. The first was that key district personnel, especially the incumbent Superintendent, anticipated the early childhood "boom" that was to flourish nationally within the next few years; the Superintendent's close ties with educational and political figures in Washington, D.C., including the planners of Head Start, strengthened his belief that a strong early childhood unit was a necessary component of any sophisticated school system. The second and more specific reason behind the creation of ECE was the District's preoccupation with its racial integration efforts. District officials and sympathetic school board members came to believe that integration would have the best chance of succeeding if it could be started at the earliest possible age. The pre-ECE programs,

2. See Patricia Bourne, *Day Care Nightmare,* for a more extended discussion of the role of the public schools in providing childcare services in California.

especially the Parent-nurseries, were not highly integrated, and it was felt that a centralized unit would facilitate their integration.

THE MARGINALITY OF ECE

In some respects, ECE seems to represent the top of the status ladder in childcare programming. It is affiliated with a prestigious school system. Some of its programs have received nationwide attention as "exemplary childcare systems."[3] Individuals on its staff are involved in statewide discussions of planned childcare services. Nevertheless, if we look at this organization in relation to the larger system of which it is a part, the BUSD, we see that ECE has an uncertain role. Just as I have earlier characterized early childhood education as a "weak" or marginal profession, so I will now argue that ECE is a "marginal" organization.[4]

The most fundamental reason for ECE's marginality within the school district is, quite simply, that preschool programs are not governed by compulsory education laws: school districts are not required to make them universally available. Thus, in spite of the enthusiasm with which the district created ECE, its personnel are constantly wary: they fear that in times of budgetary crisis, preschool programs, like other "extras" among district offerings, will be the "first cut, last funded."

But even in periods of sustained budgetary support from the district, ECE's sense of insecurity persists.[5] The trouble it has in feeling that it really "belongs" in the district gives us an interesting insight into the problems of integrating a preschool component in a modern school system. Neither of ECE's major programs, the Children's Centers or the Parent-nurseries, fit easily into mainstream public education. The all-day Children's Centers, although they purport to offer an educational component, carry the inevitable taint of custodial "daycare"; the Parent-nurseries have their roots in the more elite tradition of nursery education, yet that tradition has always prided itself on its separateness from public schooling. In both cases, because of the age of the children being served and the "irregular" backgrounds and practices of staff,

3. This designation as "exemplary" was made by the Office of Economic Opportunity. See Abt Associates, *A Study in Child Care.*

4. My approach to educational units as marginal or "insecure" draws upon the work of Burton Clark. See his *Adult Education in Transition: A Study of Institutional Insecurity,* and, especially, "Organizational Adaptation and Precarious Values."

5. In 1967-1968, there were 695 children enrolled in ECE programs; in 1973-1974, there were 864 children.

ECE leaders feel that their programs are perceived as little more than babysitting operations. The physical separation of ECE administrative offices from the central district offices accentuates the organization's feelings of isolation. As one ECE supervisor said of the central administration: "Sometimes they seem to forget we exist."

From its inception, therefore, the impulses of ECE leadership have been to upgrade the status of their organization, and to gain for it a more secure footing within the District. An early manifestation of this was the concerted and ultimately successful struggle to get credentialed ECE teaching staff placed on the district's regular salary and tenure scale. Similarly, another early goal was acquisition of new building sites, in order to expand ECE programs. This campaign, conducted chiefly through politicking at school board meetings, drew heavily on public support, especially from the new organization's parent-clients.[6] But another focus of the leadership's efforts at upward mobility was internal—to convince lower echelons of staff to take themselves more seriously as educators. As the original director of ECE recounted her "pep talks" to staff in the organization's founding period: "I encouraged staff to professionalize themselves. . .to join unions—that was the only way they would ever get salary increases. . . . The problem was that the Children's Center staff themselves thought of themselves as caretakers, not as educators. It was a real coup when I got Rachel S., who had just gotten her M.A. at Stanford, to take over Alva Children's Center—here was this educator going to run a Children's Center! It was a breakthrough in morale for the staff, and we also got a lot of public mileage out of it."

"Client Dependency" And The Parent-Nursery

The empirical portion of this study took place in ECE's Parent-nursery program. A look at the complex organization of this program suggests why the delivery of publicly funded childcare has been characterized as the "daycare nightmare." Funding for the Parent-nursery comes from state and federal, as well as local, sources; funding is thus subject to fluctuations even when BUSD support remains stable. Jurisdiction for the Parent-nurseries is overlapping and ambiguously divided between state educational and social welfare agencies, and

---

6. For an account of the emergence of Parent-nursery clients as a factor in BUSD politics, as well as a general history of the District's integration efforts, see Carole Sibley, *Never a Dull Moment: The History of a School District Attempting To Meet the Challenge of Change*.

between local and state offices of each bureaucracy.[7] Because of this confusion of authority, the Parent-nursery program has consistently been faced with complicated, sudden shifts in regulations concerning licensing of facilities, administrative procedures, staffing requirements, client eligibility, and so forth. One consequence of these complex and rather precarious arrangements, as I will explain, is the program's unusual degree of dependence on its clients.

The Parent-nursery program is actually a combination of two separate preschool programs: the District's own Parent-nursery program, which had originally been administered through the Adult School, and the state Preschool Education Program for "disadvantaged" children (A.B. 1331). Most California school districts operate a separate "1331" program; Berkeley is unusual in that it fused its "1331" offering with an existing program. The motivation for this combined program was to achieve racial and socioeconomic integration at the preschool level. In Berkeley, most of the "original Parent-nursery" participants are white and most of the "1331" participants are black.

There are thus two different funding agreements for the Parent-nursery program, each stipulating a different set of expectations of parent-clients. Adults in the "original Parent-nursery" are *obliged* to participate in the programs for a specified number of hours per week; if they do not, their children may be dropped from the program. This is because the nurseries are, technically, an adult education "course" for which the parents are enrolled; funding for the programs is based on *adult* average daily attendance. "1331" parents, on the other hand, are "strongly encouraged" to participate but are not required to do so. Monies for the "1331" program initially were exclusively based on the hours of *children's* attendance. For several years, the Parent-nurseries faced the awkward situation of requiring participation from one set of parents and only "requesting" it from another. Recently, ECE has been able to arrange to collect funds for "1331" adult participation as well. Although "1331" parents, upon registration, agree informally to participate, no "1331" child can be dropped from a nursery because its parents refuse to participate.

At first glance, the Parent-nursery situation seems rather peculiar: a program allegedly for children is funded largely on the volume of adult participation. This arrangement may seem less strange when we recall the enormous ambivalence that exists about extra-familial care for very young children. One way to guard against a potential disruption of

---

7. Bourne, *Day Care Nightmare*, pp. 21-23; 38-41.

parental authority is to bring parents into the program, as the Parent-nurseries do. The structure of the Parent-nursery, from the staff's perspective, represents a striking case of "client dependency." One-half of the program's very existence is contingent upon the voluntary participation of clients. The "1331" portion is not so drastically tied to adult participation, but because preschool programs are not compulsory, the nurseries are still ultimately dependent upon parent satisfaction. If "1331" parents were to become indifferent to the program, the nurseries would lose revenues and ECE would lose favor within the BUSD for failing to maintain integrated programs. The extreme vulnerability to clients that exists in the Parent-nursery will be discussed later as another indication of the "weakness" of early childhood professionals.

My personal observations of ECE were focused on one of its administrative units, the Bayside Cluster, which consists of four Parent-nurseries. Each of these nurseries has a morning and an afternoon session, each conducted by a head teacher and an assistant teacher. Thus, the personnel with which we will be concerned are sixteen classroom teachers (fifteen female and one male) and their supervisor, who is a member of ECE's five-woman decentralized administration.*

THE ADMINISTRATOR

Esther, the supervisor of the Bayside Cluster, is a dynamic woman in her late forties. She serves as a link between the circumscribed world of the individual Parent-nurseries and the central BUSD administration. Along with other members of ECE's administration, she represents the organization's interests in meetings with district officials, and conveys, to interested parties, reports of activities in ECE programs. Along with the teachers under her supervision, she interprets current district politics and policies, particularly as they affect the fortunes of early childhood programs. Another of her roles in relation to the teaching staff is to direct their in-service training, a prescribed bi-weekly series of educational sessions lasting several hours. A more routine and often unpleasant aspect of her job is to oversee Cluster "business": this includes negotiations with staff over such problems as faulty bus schedules, supply cutbacks, and ever-changing policies on teacher substitutions; above all, it means prodding reluctant teachers into filling out the seemingly endless number of forms demanded by district, state, and county offices. Finally, she must be available to discuss with her staff

*All names of persons and schools used in the text have been changed.

the more substantive problems that occur within the Parent-nurseries, such as particularly difficult children or poor adult participation.

Esther has a somewhat more "elite" educational background than most of her staff. She did undergraduate work at a prestigious Midwestern university, and received an M.A. in education from the University of California. Her graduate training and much of her own teaching experience was in primary, as well as preschool, education. Much of her considerable knowledge about the unique aspects of preschool programming, and her familiarity with the vast child development literature, comes from the immense amount of reading she manages to squeeze into her crowded schedule.

Her lifestyle is, by Berkeley standards, a rather conventional one. She lives in a comfortable middle-class neighborhood with her husband, an academic, and her children. She has, however, a skilled capacity to move comfortably in the various social worlds of Berkeley, and she seems equally at ease with district bureaucrats, her own quite diverse teaching staff, and different groups of ECE parents, ranging from staid middle-class blacks to freewheeling white communards.

Esther's sense of the larger political context in which individual Parent-nursery programs operate is an important difference between herself and her staff. Unlike most of the classroom teachers, she routinely attends the district's weekly board meetings, whether ECE-related matters are scheduled or not; in the middle of a heavy work week, it is not unusual for her to remain at such meetings until past midnight. Through her many informal friendship ties in the District hierarchy, she seems to manage well the considerable task of keeping abreast of the complex inner life of district politics.

Her sense of the "larger picture" extends to national as well as local events. She keeps closely in touch with trends in early childhood education, as well as the childcare scene more generally. Like many others in early childhood education, she is rather scornful of social workers, especially their efforts to provide preschool services. Partially because of this hostility to the dominant social work tradition of childcare services, she is very ambivalent about "daycare," although ECE itself administers all-day Children's Centers for working parents. But in spite of her strong self-image as a professional educator, she sees the mandate of ECE as going beyond a narrowly defined "educational" program for children; she is deeply committed to integrating families into ECE programs, and work with parents and relatives is almost as important to her as work with the children themselves.

THE TEACHERS

The Bayside teachers are an interracial group—nine whites and seven blacks—ranging in age from the early twenties to the late forties. Their primary responsibility is to run a "program" at their assigned nursery schools. While they meet periodically with their supervisor to establish "program goals," until very recently, finding the means for reaching these goals has been left largely to them. Each Parent-nursery, while in certain basic ways resembling the others, also reflects the particular personalities and interests of its own staff.

In addition to work with children, a significant component of the teaching staff's responsibility is work with parents. First of all, they have to regulate and maintain parent attendance. During the course of the school session itself, parents have to be integrated into ongoing activities and be allocated specific duties. A more formal part of work with adults is the parent education program, a bi-monthly series of evening meetings. As with the children's portion of the program, there is no centrally determined notion of parent education, and teachers have considerable leeway in defining the content of these meetings.

Other aspects of the classroom staff's responsibilities include annual home visits with each participating family; periodic individual conferences with parents at school; the administering, twice a year, of state-required tests to each child; and "tutorial" work (additional hours of individualized instruction) with children from the "1331" segment of the program.

Finally, the Bayside staff spend what they consider to be an excessive amount of time in meetings. There is a weekly Cluster meeting, which alternates between in-service and "business" meetings. There are periodic meetings scheduled with the ECE psychologist and health consultant. There are meetings scheduled with representatives from the county and state social welfare departments to discuss the "1331" children in the program. There are, in addition, innumerable "special" meetings with various central district personnel—such as meetings to discuss new testing procedures or new "multiethnic curriculum" recommendations. Many of the Bayside staff, moreover, pursue some educational coursework while they are working.

And so although the Parent-nursery program itself is only a half-day one, the Bayside teachers always seem to feel overworked. Even when things are "normal," they complain of the difficulty of reconciling endless meetings and bureaucratic responsibilities with the amount of time they would ideally want to spend on classroom preparation. Crises—such as a problem with an exceptionally difficult child or an emergency in a participating family—of course absorb even more time and energy, and increase the pressure the teachers normally feel. To generalize, we might say that most of the Bayside teachers seem to find their work enjoyable and challenging, but tiring.

The Bayside teachers have varied educational and teaching backgrounds. The fairly open educational requirements for Parent-nursery positions—a California teaching credential for head teacher, two years of college, with some educational course work, for assistant teacher —allowed ECE to recruit from a broad base at the time of its organizational expansion in 1965. Many of the current staff were initially recruited from among parent participants in existing nurseries. The original director of ECE specifically sought persons with a school-teaching background who had young children of their own.

Only a minority of the Bayside teachers were originally trained exclusively in preschool education. Interestingly enough, this minority includes some of both the youngest and the oldest staff members in ECE: Naomi Nathanson, for example, a white head teacher, came to Berkeley fifteen years ago after having received an M.A. in early childhood development at one of the most prestigious nursery school institutes in the East; Daisy Carter, a young black assistant teacher, came to the Parent-nursery program in 1971 after studying early childhood education at a Bay Area community college. Others on the staff came predominantly from elementary school backgrounds, which in some cases included training in preschool education. One staff member had been trained as a physical education teacher, and another as a home economics teacher. One had taught high school in the South.

In spite of their diverse backgrounds, after assuming their jobs at ECE, the staff have been obliged to undertake considerable course work in early childhood education. This experience, most of it at local colleges and universities, has apparently been successful in giving the staff a strong sense of nursery school traditions. Although, as we shall see, some of them are beginning to question parts of this tradition, most of them fully understand and accept such classic nursery principles as the primacy of "socio-emotional development" and "creative play."

The lifestyles of the Bayside teachers are diverse. Most (ten) are married, some are divorced, and a handful have never been married. Most live with husbands or children in conventional nuclear households, but the two youngest teachers—both white—live communally, and some black staff live in more extended family settings. The wide range of occupations of the married teachers' spouses shows how hard it is to generalize about the social class position of this group as a whole. The husbands include a psychologist, a minister, an insurance man, a self-employed businessman, a skilled laborer, a service worker, a poverty program executive, and one man who, during the period of this study, was an unemployed teacher and worked at odd jobs. In terms of the husband's income, and the family's place of residence, the whites as a group seemed more solidly placed in the middle class than the blacks; yet the white married group also included the unemployed teacher and the self-employed businessman whose sporadic earnings made the family dependent upon the wife as the major wage-earner.

A common point that links these otherwise diverse households is their involvement in the Berkeley schools, as parents as well as employees. Of the twelve teachers in the Cluster who have children, eleven live in Berkeley and send their children to local schools. This is useful for these teachers on several grounds: first, it gives them an experience of the "other side" of the parent-teacher relationship; second, they are introduced to other parts of the larger system of which their small and rather isolated nurseries are a part.

The Bayside teaching staff has a different relationship to the political issues facing ECE than does Esther, their administrator. Involved as they are in the everyday effort to run a successful program, the classroom teachers have less opportunity to explore the larger political picture and less sense of how to act upon it. Although they are not politically active on a regular basis, the staff does become readily mobilized in periods of crisis, as when cutbacks in ECE programming are threatened.

The extent of continuing self-education among the staff varies greatly. Some of the teachers are avid readers of child development literature, especially the works of Piaget and his followers; most seem to prefer more practical reading matter, such as journal articles on the design of special curriculum projects. Others say with regret that they simply have no time for reading much of anything. Unlike Esther, none of the Bayside teachers are members of the major professional association of early childhood educators, the National Association for the Education of Young Children.

Only a few of the Bayside teachers are closely in touch with childcare developments on the national scale, though virtually all of them are favorably disposed toward childcare and are particularly sympathetic to

the needs of working mothers. Yet these teachers remain confused about
the relationship between "childcare" and their own field of early
childhood education. Like their supervisor, many of these nursery
teachers feel that "childcare" carries the taint of the "daycare"
programs of social workers.

To conclude, we can see a number of differences between the
Bayside supervisor and the teaching staff. Esther is more "intellectual," the staff on the whole is more pragmatic. Much of Esther's
energy is directed toward broad "political" questions; most of the
staff's energies are focused on carrying out a meaningful daily program.
Esther has a more developed "professional" orientation, and a greater
sense of shared interests with early educators elsewhere; the teachers are
more involved in the personal lives of their clients. Though the bulk of
this study will be devoted to examining encounters between "professionals" and clients, these differences between Esther and her staff
remind us of the importance of noting internal tensions as well. How
ECE as a whole responds to the demands of clients and other relevant
constituencies is determined, in many ways, by the character of the
internal negotiations between administrators, who have one set of
understandings, and classroom practitioners, who have another.

Let us look more closely at the teachers in whose schools most of the
classroom observations took place. Sarah Lewis (white) and Lucy Isaac
(black) are the head teacher and assistant teacher, respectively, at
Cottage Parent-nursery, in the three-year-old class; Celia Jones (black)
and Jane Selden (white) are the head and assistant teachers at Park
Parent-nursery, in the four-year-old class.

Sarah

Sarah is a slightly plump, red-cheeked woman in her early forties
who looks like—and in many ways *is*—the archtypal nursery school
teacher, an identity she cherishes. To parents, she has a baffling ability
to make herself "child-like," and yet at other times make the children
more "grown-up." In the course of the school day, she will enter fully
into the play of the children, participating as well as supervising; at the
end of the day, however, she will gather her group of twenty-five
three-year-olds around her in a circle, and very seriously review the
highlights of the day and orient the group to the following day's
activities. She identifies strongly with "old-time" nursery school traditions and is among those Bayside teachers who are most upset by client
and administrative pressures to move from a "socio-emotional"-based

program to a more "cognitive" one. Her grounding in such nursery principles as "emotional well-being" and "social development" is shown in the following statement she made at a staff meeting, in which she summed up her goals for three-year-olds: "I want the kids to be able to leave their mothers, I want them to be able to divorce themselves from their parents' anxieties. . . . I want them to learn skills with toys and games—for example, I want them to learn what size tricycle they can handle. . . . I want them to learn to initiate friendship, I want them to have group skills."

Sarah does not draw very firm boundaries between her job and her private life. She periodically involves her husband and children in nursery activity: her husband leads the children in gymnastics, and her own teenagers more generally help out. She makes more home visits than technically required, and grows to know some of the participating families quite well. She has, over the years, built up friendly ties with the residents of the community in which Cottage is located; she proudly tells of the neighbor ("He doesn't even know my name; I don't know his") who spontaneously offered her the loan of a rooster as a pet for the school.

She is ideologically committed to parent participation, but concedes that working with parents sometimes makes her nervous. She gets along very well with some parents, not so well with others. In any event, dealing with a large group of parents, as at an evening Parents' Meeting, is a chronic source of anxiety for her. Not unlike the earlier generations of nursery school teachers described by Margaret Mead,[8] Sarah seems most at home in the world of children.

Lucy

Lucy is a gracious and gentle Southern woman, also in her early forties. Her calmness and stability make a good counterweight to Sarah's fancifulness. Those parents, especially blacks, who find communication at times difficult with Sarah because they see her as too far gone into the world of children, find in Lucy a down-to-earth and sympathetic listener. She was first recruited into the ECE staff while participating with her own child in a Parent-nursery program. Since joining the staff, she has taken much course work in early childhood education, but she seems much less bound to nursery school orthodoxy than Sarah. For example, like other of her black colleagues, she is not

8. Margaret Mead, *The School in American Culture*, pp. 26-27.

opposed to the idea of some basic skill instruction taking place in the nursery.

Her special commitment in the program is helping black children and their families. She sees one function of a preschool program as the preparation, in a variety of ways, for elementary school; her fervent hope is that the Cottage experience will help break the pattern of educational failure of black children in Berkeley. She also feels herself to be a special advocate of the black parents in the program—both in their dealings with ECE and with other agencies. Her particularly strong interest in black children and parents, however, does not keep her from being attentive and concerned with whites. Parents and children of both races develop strong bonds with her and refer to her as "almost a member of our family."

Lucy does draw a sharper line between work and private life than Sarah does. She is very engrossed in her own family, and jealously tries to protect the amount of time she can spend with them. She good-naturedly grumbles about the hours she is obliged to spend in meetings and in classes.

Celia

The teaching team at Park is not such a well-balanced one. Both Celia and Jane are excellent in work with young children, but both are insecure in their work with adults. Celia, originally from the South, is in her late thirties. She is attractive and good-humored, though often quite shy, except when with children. Her style with the children is a bit more formal than Sarah's; rather than entering fully into the world of the child, she remains close by, as a very friendly adult. She is firm but affectionate with the children and seems to enjoy her job most when she is supervising their play. Her college training in the South was in elementary education; though she has subsequently had additional early childhood course work, like Lucy, she is not strongly indoctrinated with classic nursery school teachings. In fact, for some time, Celia has quietly incorporated into her program traces of "academic" instruction. Her willingness to have some form of basic skill learning at Park —though this went against Parent-nursery tradition—is largely due to the special obligation she feels toward the black children and parents in her program. Such instruction is given not only in response to the demands of black parents; Celia herself believes that some familiarity with language and arithmetic will be useful to her four-year-olds who will be shortly entering "real" school.

Celia's relations with parents are of mixed quality, and the part of her job she acknowledges to be the most difficult. Like her colleagues, she relates well to individual parents but feels uncomfortable dealing with parents as a group. Her relationships with blacks at Park are among the most gratifying—and, in some cases, the most difficult—of her parent contacts. With some of the younger black women, in particular, she develops unusually strong ties, dispensing advice and encouragement in matters that go far beyond the boundaries of the nursery. Celia, as we shall see, is a central figure in the Parent-nursery's mostly hidden informal helping network. With other blacks, however, her relations are more strained. As head teacher, it is her job to monitor parent attendance hours; because black parents at Park are among the most irregular participants, she is placed in the difficult situation of having to confront the non-attenders and at the same time placate a few irate whites who claim that the Parent-nursery maintains a double standard of parent participation.[9] It is an awkward task, made even more difficult by Celia's shyness.

Jane

Jane, in her late twenties, is energetic, giggly, and somewhat nervous. She has a Master's degree in early childhood education, which makes her among the most educated of all the teachers in the Cluster, heads as well as assistants. She is particularly noted for her imaginative contributions to Park's curriculum: she initiates novel art projects, helps the children to fashion extraordinary costumes, and designs special "learning skill" projects based on Piagetian principles.

Of the four teachers we shall be observing in depth, Jane arouses the most controversy among parents. While everyone acknowledges her talent in designing classroom activities, some parents find her personally to be "disorganized" and "just a kid herself." She connects better with other parents, however, and has established friendships with some that continue past the parents' tenure in the nursery. Her most successful relations with parents are built around mutual interests in art, pottery, and other crafts. Jane is acutely aware of the difficulties she has in establishing authority with some parents, and partly because of this, she is hesitant to demand a transfer to a head teacher position, even though she is educationally qualified for one.

9. Technically speaking, the disgruntled white parents were correct. Unlike children participating under the "Parent-nursery" component of the program, "1331" children could not be dropped from the program because of their parents' non-participation.

Though she does not usually get as deeply involved as Celia in emergency situations facing Park parents, she too will intervene when appropriate. When the situation demands it, she will readily shed her "child-like" persona and counsel a troubled parent. On occasion, she will arrange for an informal meeting between her husband, a psychologist, and a parent.

THE PARENTS

Each of the Parent-nursery classes enrolls from twenty to twenty-five families at any given time. Thus, in the course of observing the morning class at Cottage and the afternoon class at Park, I encountered more than forty families. Though the situation was different at other nurseries in the Bayside Cluster, all the regular participants at Park and Cottage during this study were women (fathers and other males, however, occasionally participated on a temporary basis). Hence in reporting my observation of these classes, I will use the words "parents" and "mothers" interchangeably.

How can the reader best get a sense of the forty or so participating mothers? One way would be to compare the Cottage parents to those at Park; the somewhat different characters of these schools are in some respect due to the different parent populations at each. Another way would be to divide parents for comparative purposes along the lines suggested by the funding arrangements of the schools themselves: between the "Parent-nursery" mothers, who enroll through Adult Education courses, pay a small fee, and are committed to a certain number of participation hours; and the "1331" mothers, whose designation as "past, present, or potential" welfare recipients entitles their children, by state law, to a preschool program. A third way—the one I will use in this book—is to compare parents along racial lines, which to some degree parallels the previous approach, inasmuch as most of the white participants are "Parent-nursery" and most of the blacks are "1331." Comparing by race, I believe, is the most useful way of getting to some of the key conflicts among Parent-nursery clients.

A racial comparison is not without its limitations. I recognize that some of the parental differences that I will be discussing in terms of race have been analyzed by others along class lines.[10] Moreover, comparing

10. See Melvin L. Kohn, *Class and Conformity: A Study in Values*, and "Social Class and Parental Values."

these two groups by race obscures the fact that within each group there are differences of income and lifestyle. This is especially true of a small white "hip" parent contingent, whose reactions to the Parent-nursery resemble neither those of the middle-class whites nor those of the black parents—even though the white "hip" parents are of a similar income level to most blacks in the program.

In spite of these shortcomings, a racial comparison seemed to me the best approach because the participants themselves categorize the adults in the Parent-nursery according to race. In conversations with parents of either race, references were constantly made to "black parents" and "white parents"—not to differences of class or lifestyle. This tendency to divide the school into black and white is doubtless intensified by the schools' two funding sources, which tend to follow racial lines. An additional factor, I believe, is the climate of opinion in the Berkeley community—and especially in its schools—in which integration, and its difficult career, is a matter of constant public debate.

In the following sections, I will offer some general introductory remarks about each group of parents, with the hope that more of their individual personalities will emerge in subsequent chapters.

White Parents

Of the more than twenty-five or so whites observed during this study, all but five or six are married and, on the basis of their husbands' occupations, can be called middle class. Some of these occupations are doctor and lawyer, city planner, architect, professor, schoolteacher, psychiatrist, engineer, businessman, and graduate student. The women in this group are essentially homebound young mothers, with slightly less than half having children even younger than their preschoolers. Only one in this group has a part-time job (at a University laboratory); a few others take a college course or two during the hours when their children are in nursery school.

The lifestyles of these young families can be called "Berkeley liberal," a term which here includes a cultural as well as a political component. They are not rooted in the "freak" culture of Telegraph Avenue or in the radical political movements of the community, yet their lives incorporate some elements of each. Their relationship to the counterculture is reflected mainly in their deep interest in developing craft skills, learning to bake bread and prepare other natural foods, and pursuing "hip" styles of dress. Politically, none identify themselves as "radicals": several engage, or have in the past, in anti-war activity, civil rights, ecological and consumer politics, and in local Berkeley elections, usually working for left-liberal candidates.

The women's movement is an important but troubling issue for these middle-class mothers. They are responsive to some aspects of the movement, but they are quite uncomfortable with what they see as its preoccupation with issues of work and careers. The movement's repeated stress on the fact that about 40 percent of all American women work also means, of course, that 60 percent do *not* — and these Parent-nursery mothers are among them. They are at home in an era in which it is increasingly awkward, in many Berkeley circles, to be "just a housewife." Awareness of the sudden unfashionableness of the house-wife role, predictably, generates much ambivalence about the women's movement. On the one hand, there is defensiveness and anger at those "women's libbers" who allegedly devalue the homemaker.[11] On the other hand, there is an undeniable current of interest in the movement, especially on the part of those who openly acknowledge feelings of restlessness with their current situation.

Only about five or six single white women on welfare, whom I call white "hip," were encountered during this study. They are more irregular about their own nursery participation than the middle-class whites, and are apt to abruptly withdraw their children from the program before the semester's end. The lifestyle of this group is more unconventional than that of other parents in the nursery: some live alone with their children, some live communally, some live in apartments with male partners. In comparison with the middle-class whites' selectivity, it is members of this "hip" group who are most likely to participate fully in Berkeley's counterculture, by attending rock music concerts and frequenting restaurants and nightspots in the hip community, for example. While this group expresses a general sympathy with radical politics, none of its members were politically active at the time of the study. Only one of this very small sample strongly identifies with the women's

11. For various expressions of negative reactions to the women's movement that appeared in popular magazines during the time of this study, see Anne Bernays, "What Are You Supposed To Do if You Like Children?," *Atlantic,* March 1970, pp. 107-109; Joyce Brothers, "Women's Lib Backlash," *Good Housekeeping,* September 1972, pp. 54-58; *Ladies Home Journal,* "Women's Lib and Me," November 1970, pp. 69-74; *McCall's,* "What McCall's Readers Think about Women's Liberation," March 1971, pp. 68-70; and Judith Viorst, "What Worries Me Most about Women's Lib," *Redbook,* May 1974, pp. 51-53. All the above make specific reference to the premium placed by the women's movement on out-of-home "careers."

movement, but none of the others exhibit such mixed feelings as do the middle-class group.

Although white "hip" parents at any given moment form only a small minority of a Parent-nursery class, their impact is felt beyond their numbers. Their proclivity to express their likes and dislikes forcefully make them a faction to be reckoned with among other parents and teachers alike.

Black Parents

Most of the twenty-odd black families observed in this study are enrolled through the "1331" program and thus come from low-income households. Some are welfare recipients; a slightly higher proportion can be classified as "working poor." Among the approximately ten who are married and living with husbands, the husbands' occupations include: skilled and unskilled laborer, gas station attendant, factory worker, and (in the most solidly middle-class of black families in the sample) a chemist working for the Army. In comparison with the white group, the blacks at the Parent-nurseries are more firmly rooted in the Bay Area; most were born and raised there, while others came from the South at an early age with their families of origin.

Another major racial difference is that some among the black group—approximately six at any one time—themselves hold full-time jobs. Participation obligations to the nursery are met either by kin or by hired babysitters. This practice, especially when it involves hired babysitters, does stretch program rules, but the organization deals with these unorthodox arrangements mostly by looking the other way. Some of the jobs of the working mothers are: cannery worker, secretary, poverty-program aide, and high-school aide.

Still another difference from the white women, especially the middle-class parents, is that the black parents are less preoccupied with the women's movement; in fact, they are somewhat skeptical of it. This seems consistent with the frequent observation that the women's movement has not broken out of its white, middle-class base. The skepticism of this particular group of blacks may also reflect a less idealized relationship to the world of work: in fact, a group of these women *were* working, but at low-paying, often tiring "jobs," and not "careers." But if there is less explicit interest in the women's movement, there is, in comparison with the whites, a heightened interest in race and racism, both in society at large and in the Parent-nursery in particular.

Since the black women involved in the Parent-nurseries cover a much greater age span than the whites—participants range from teenagers to grandmothers—it is, of course, much harder to generalize about this group's lifestyles. One observation I can offer is that this group's cultural and social life intersects only slightly with Berkeley's counter-culture and is more firmly rooted in institutions of the black community, such as churches, clubs, and neighborhood organizations. Some of the blacks are politically active, working, for example, in local electoral campaigns.

A final impressionistic point to be made about the black participants—one for which there is no substantive data—is that they are "poor" but not "hard-core" poor. There is a certain sense of "mobility" among these women—both those who are working and those who are at home—that differentiate them from others who might have similar incomes. This psychological, rather than economic, classification of black participants was frequently made by ECE staff. As the community worker, whose primary task is recruitment, told some ECE administrators: "You're not getting the 'down-and-outs' into this program. They're the ones who can't handle participation, who sometimes can't even get their kids onto the bus." The apparently self-selected "upwardly mobile" character of its black clients is, to a limited extent, seen as a problem by ECE. As one supervisor said: "We may not be reaching those families who need our programs most."

THE RESEARCH SITES: "PARK" AND "COTTAGE"

Park and Cottage, the two Parent-nurseries in which I did classroom observations, have quite different personalities, not only because of the differing styles of their teaching teams, but also because of their respective traditions, or lack of them. Park, which is a refurbished, sprawling old Victorian house, is a Berkeley "institution." It is located not far from the University, adjacent to a popular, outdoor community recreation area; even when the Parent-nursery is not in session, many of the parents and children congregate in the area. Much of Park's "mystique" comes from a history of periodic district attempts to close it down (as a cost-saving measure), which have been countered in each case by successful "Save Park" campaigns mounted by staff, parents, and even "alumnae" parents. Virtually all of the white families at Park live in the immediate neighborhood, and most parents walk their children to school each day. However, the popularity of the Park recreation area and the whites' sense of the nursery itself as a "neighborhood institution" serves to accentuate feelings of racial separation at the school. None of the blacks at Park live in the neighborhood. Most of the black children and participating mothers arrive by schoolbus, though some come by car. Few of the blacks make use of the area on weekends or holidays. Park, therefore, is white turf.

Cottage Parent-nursery, in Berkeley's flatlands, is not a community institution in the sense that Park is. It, too, is part of a larger recreational facility, but an indoor one, used mainly by neighborhood teenagers and not by either Cottage parents. or children. A few of the participating black families live in the immediate neighborhood and walk their children to school; everyone else arrives by bus or carpool. We might speculate that one possible benefit of Cottage's lack of mystique is that all participants approach it as neutral—Cottage is neither black nor white territory.

The organization of events at each Parent-nursery is basically similar. Sessions last three hours and are a mixture of pre-planned activities and free play. There are usually several projects occurring at once—art, music, or cooking—and children are free to choose any one of these or to play freely indoors or outdoors. Both schools serve the traditional juice and crackers each day at an appointed time, and for the most part, this snack time is the only fixed event in an otherwise fluid schedule.

At each Parent-nursery, parents are expected to participate at one school session per week, and to attend the bi-monthly evening meetings. What parents actually did at the nursery was a matter for negotiation between them and the teachers. The most common form is for the parent simply to arrive at the school on her appointed day and be given an assignment by the teacher—to supervise a particular play area, for example. In some instances, parents are requested in advance by teachers to prepare for a special activity to be done with the children on the parent's participation day. Sometimes mothers themselves prepare special projects beforehand—sometimes informing the teachers in advance, sometimes not. Whatever the parent's specific responsibility, a general expectation of all parents is that they will also help in monitoring the entire school—that is, break up fights, reach out to particularly isolated children, and so forth. All parents are expected to help in clean-up activity at the end of each session.

Finally, in spite of their status as "schools," and in spite of affiliation with a large, centralized bureaucracy, Park and Cottage manage to sustain an informal, almost "family-like" quality that seems most unusual in a modern urban school system. This spirit is manifested in various ways: the parents, coming early to pick up their children, who feel free to come into the nursery and chat with staff and other parents; the cordial relations between janitors and matrons and the children, staff, and parents, and the janitors inclusion in many nursery events; the parents who, on their participation days, routinely bring along kin, ranging from newly born infants to teenage nephews to grandmothers; the teachers who quietly provide lunch at school for a child whose mother has been ill. The rigid distinctions between "school," "family," and "community" that exist in most educational systems become pleasantly blurred in these Parent-nurseries.

THE RESEARCH ISSUES

In the following chapters I will report on the research I did in Berkeley's Parent-nurseries. The heart of this research was twice-weekly observations at Park and Cottage during the school-year 1971-1972, and, more irregularly, during 1972-1973. I also regularly attended the weekly staff meetings of the Bayside Cluster during 1971-1972, and, more occasionally, during 1972-1973. I conducted interviews with the Bayside teachers, with ECE supervisors, and with other ECE and district personnel. During the summer of 1972, I interviewed twenty parents—eleven white, eight black, and one Japanese-American—from Park and Cottage, at their homes. During the period of this research, I regularly attended the school board meetings of the BUSD whenever an item pertaining to ECE was on the agenda.

There were two key issues with which I was concerned in my research: first, the conduct of negotiations between providers and users of professionalized childcare over what such a service ought to be; and, second, how these negotiations are affected when childcare is delivered under the auspices of the public schools. My view of early childhood educators, to recapitulate, is that they are "weak" but upwardly mobile professionals, who desire a greater level of legitimacy and autonomy. In studying the Parent-nurseries, I was able to examine how these aspirations of early childhood professionals are received by a diverse client group, whose expectations about childcare differ not only from those of the educators but also from those of fellow clients. Chapters Three through Six explore the relationship of the Bayside staff to each of its client groups, and the new definitions of early childhood programs which seemed to be emerging from these encounters. Chapter Seven, the conclusion of this work, is a reconsideration of some of the theoretical issues about childcare policy which were raised in Chapter One.

3

What Early Childhood Professionals Want from Their Clients

Early childhood educators, like other professionals, want clients to make regular use of their services and to acknowledge their claims to expertise. But the clients' own doubts about the value of "professionalized childcare," and the fact that their participation in this care is required, combine to make it difficult for ECE staff members to achieve these desires. The daily presence of parents in ECE facilities, performing largely the same tasks as the teachers, weakens the claim that normally belongs to professionals: the ability to perform services the clients cannot.

The special set of circumstances facing ECE workers leads them to make two possibly conflicting demands on clients. Most fundamentally, of course, they want parents to meet the obligation to participate; without this participation, there would be no programs. Yet they also want something more from parents. They want acknowledgment as *educators:* as professionals who have specialized insights into young children, and whose intervention can make a real difference in children's development. The Parent-nursery staff's relationship with clients is thus essentially an emotional balancing act: parents must be treated graciously, and deferred to when necessary—but not at too great a cost to the self-esteem of the would-be "professionals."

This chapter explores the ways in which Berkeley's early childhood educators manage their dependency on clients. I will show that an official ideology favoring parent "partnership" has developed—an ideology which is a functional adaptation to the actual necessity of assuring client presence. But because massive client involvement threatens professional authority, I will also discuss the impulses the staff members feel, ideology notwithstanding, to differentiate themselves from parent-clients, and to preserve their identities as "educators." This chapter will outline the four roles in which teachers must work with parents: parents as teachers, as students, as recipients of social services, and as political colleagues. I will suggest that the tensions which reach their height when professionals and parents interact in the classroom are somewhat mitigated as the two groups undertake joint political activity on behalf of the organization.

PARENTS AS "TEACHERS": IDEOLOGY AND REALITY

What does parent participation in a professionally run children's institution mean? It is possible to conceptualize parent participation as a continuum ranging from total parent control to complete subservience to professionals. On one end of this continuum are "parents' coopera- tives" in which parents themselves establish schools, sit on the board of directors, hire and fire staff members, or actually perform all staff functions themselves. Traditionally, such cooperatives have been most prevalent at the preschool level (another indication of the early childhood professionals' status difficulties), but lately this model is becoming more common at the elementary and secondary school levels with the growth of "alternative" or "free" schools.[1] At the other extreme of the parent participation continuum is the use of parents as paid or volunteer "aides" in public schools. The recent use of aides appears to have evolved mainly as a response to increasing discipline problems in schools, and even when aides are called upon to perform teaching functions, they are still clearly subordinate to the classroom teacher. Under the first model of parent participation, parents literally control the school and professionals are present as hired staff members;

1. On parental involvement in free schools, see Allen Graubard, *Free the Children: Radical Reform and the Free School Movement.*

in the other, parents are totally without formal powers and receive instructions from administrative personnel and teachers. A key difference between the two models is the amount of ease a parent feels in initiating and directing activities with the children, independently of the teacher.

ECE's interpretation of parent participation seems to fall on a middle ground between these two models. The "aide" model of public schools is loudly repudiated: "Our parents are *not* aides," ECE teachers emphasize. On several occasions, I observed teachers saying to the parents, "You know, you are teachers here too." At the same time, parents in ECE programs do not have the ultimate powers of those in a private cooperative. They can neither hire nor fire teachers (although they are, to an extent, consulted about such decisions) and they do not formally make school policy (though again, they are sometimes consulted). And while they do not usually act like aides, they also fall short, in subtle but important ways, of acting out the complete role of teacher. Further, if individual parents should come too close to approximating the identity of "teacher," they will meet with staff resistance. In fact, it is partly through differentiating themselves from over-eager parents that marginal professionals, working in a very ambiguous situation, come to get a sense of their own "professionalism."

Several examples will show the subtle but firm boundaries that the teachers sought to draw between themselves and parents.

1. At a staff meeting, the Bayside cluster discussed the District's new "Guided Self-Analysis" project. In GSA, teachers videotape themselves and then evaluate their own performances; it was initially introduced to the District as a staff development program. The idea gradually emerged, however, of offering it to selected parents who would be trained to tape their interactions with their children at home and then to evaluate the material themselves. When Esther, the Bayside supervisor, enthusiastically brought this idea to her staff, the teachers were noticeably hesitant. As one said, only half-jokingly, "That's all I need! If my parents are in a District training program, no matter what it's all about, I won't be able to tell them anything."

2. The Bayside cluster had just finished presenting a public exhibition of Parent/nursery materials. Each of the teaching teams was responsible for bringing in material from their classes. Although the exhibition was ostensibly designed to reveal the entire range of Parent-nursery activities, there was only one small display, from Park, which in any way acknowledged parent involvement. The bulk of the exhibit was

teacher-designed curriculum materials. When I mentioned this to one of the teachers a few days afterward, she somewhat sheepishly said, "It really wasn't right, I guess . . . some people's egos just took over."

3. The Bayside cluster had spent several weeks of in-service meetings discussing various developmental theorists, and was in the process of deciding what to discuss next. Sylvia, the head teacher from Pacific, a school with many university-affiliated families, said, "Let's keep on going with this. Let's do more on Erikson and all of them. It's not that these discussions really help me with my teaching . . . but they're really useful for dealing with parents . . . they make me 'authoritative.' When they challenge me on something, I'll just throw Erikson at them."

Nonetheless, the official "line" on parent participation at the school sites is that it is desirable for parents to have as much autonomy and self-direction as possible. Sarah, the head teacher at Cottage, once pointed out that although it was January, "My parents are still at November; they still look to me to initiate everything. If I had had a good assistant teacher earlier this year instead of Janine, my parents would be farther along by now and wouldn't need me so much." A similar view was expressed by Esther, the Bayside supervisor, immediately after a staff meeting in which it was suggested that some teachers might take time off from the classroom to participate in District-wide teachers' committees. The suggestion was rejected by the teachers, who expressed reluctance to be absent from their classes for any length of time. Esther's comment was, "It bothers me that they don't think that by now the parents could manage without them." These and similar statements suggest that after a suitable training period, in which they learn to perform school routines, parents can undertake virtually all of the functions of a teacher—except for bureaucratic ones, such as the keeping of attendance records.

The behavior of teachers in the classroom coincides to a substantial degree with this ideology. Parents are strongly encouraged by teachers to lead activities with the children. Parents are particularly commended if they initiate projects that are not regularly part of the curriculum —such as special cooking or art projects, or bringing a special guest to the school. The staff also encourages parents to give direction to the evening meetings. In all cases observed, the staff made a genuine effort to arrange meetings that would satisfy any expressed wishes. In fact, a parent's "career" of participation within a particular school is often described by the teachers in terms of increasing amounts of self-direction. For example, Sarah once pointed out Gail R., a young black woman: "Look at her, two months ago she would come in here—when she did come, which was rarely!—and just sit. Now she brings in that puzzle from home and goes over it with the kids."

As the discussion of different models of parent participation indicates, there are many interpretations of the meaning of parent "participation." Each institution, presumably, evolves its own particular interpretation according to its own logic. There are several sources for ECE's "parents as partners" ideology. In the most general sense, this ideology helps to make ECE's programs more palatable to its host district. The "parents as partners" notion reduces the misgivings certain school board members and other key district personnel often have about school programs for very young children.

Another more immediate influence on the ECE ideology toward parent participation is the relatively low level of initial involvement (both physical and psychic) of many parents in the program. This is partly a product of the lack of initial understanding by many parents of the program's objectives. Those who join the program thinking of it as exclusively a children's program rather than one also encompassing "adult education" quite often are irregular and somewhat indifferent participants. At the beginning of school semesters (or with the individual entry of new parents at later points), the staff's task is to attempt a "conversion" process which consists of two elements: (1) to make the parent identify with the school and come to realize its dependence on her contribution; and (2) to make the parent come to enjoy participation obligations as ends in themselves. The following incident suggests the way in which teachers conceive of this conversion process, especially in terms of its first element, the parent's "essentialness."

The teacher, Sarah, is speaking to the observer about two student-teachers from a nearby state college who have been assigned to her school for field placement for two months. The observer remarks that things will be "easier, having two more adults around." Sarah's reply is, "Oh, in some ways, it will be great. I'll be more free . . . but I worry about the effect it will have on parents. I'm afraid of sibling rivalries . . . I'm afraid they will feel obsolete. I just spent *months* convincing them that we need them here and now these two will be here, doing the fancy projects they learned at State, and I just wonder how some of the parents will react to it."

Here the staff assumes that the initial hesitation of most parents is likely to be overcome if parents come to see themselves as central to the program's functioning and not merely as subordinates to the staff. This assumption helps account for the staff's general air of non-directiveness in the classroom (vis-à-vis adults) and even for their periodic references to "parents as teachers."

A final influence on the teachers' ideology about parent participation is the ambivalence that surrounds professional care of young children. This ambivalence is one that early childhood personnel themselves feel, and it contributes to contradictions in their work behavior. There are variations among individual teachers, but nearly all of those studied felt uncomfortable to some degree in interactions with parents, and in valuing their own "professional judgments" over the parent's "intuitive" ones. Again and again in parent-teacher discussions, one hears what can be seen as ritual disclaimers on the part of teachers: "Of course, you know her best, but . . ." The inevitable "natural conflict between parent and teacher" that Waller argues is characteristic of all school situations takes on a special meaning in this case, where the educators' claims to legitimacy are already so shaky.[2]

Sarah, in complaining about a certain parent at Cottage, described a very revealing case of a parent-teacher jurisdictional struggle over a child: "She's always giving food to Gerry just before school. So he comes here with the food and the other children freak out. I ask her not to do it. . . . It's subtle sabotage of me, I'm sure. She wants Gerry to be fixated on her. Do you see the way, whenever he cries, he asks where she is, if he can go home?"

Teacher ideology about parent autonomy in the classroom has to be understood in terms of this ambivalence. One might guess that for some teachers, encouraging parents to be "as much like teachers as possible" reduces the dissonance teachers feel about being in such an ambiguous situation. But whether or not all teachers feel this internal conflict about their professional prerogatives, they do seem aware enough of parental ambivalence to tread lightly in establishing their own authority. Encouragement of parent independence in the classroom is one manifestation of the teachers' awareness of their own precarious situation.

Not surprisingly, there is a discrepancy between the teachers' official ideology of "parents as partners" and the real structuring of school responsibility. This is clearly apparent from staff attitudes toward the "overly involved" parent. According to the staff's ideology, the "good" parents are those who participate regularly and in a "full " way, leading activities, initiating projects, and so forth, while the

2. Willard Waller, *The Sociology of Teaching*, p. 69.

"problem" parents are those who participate irregularly, are withdrawn, and look to teachers for guidance. But in practice, there is a fine line beyond which the "good" parent can become troublesome. The inappropriate involvement of parents, especially during school sessions, can jeopardize the children's portion of the program. One rather humorous example of this occurred one day at Park, when one of the scheduled activities was bread-baking. Though only one mother was technically assigned to supervise, the three other parents who were present that day crowded into the kitchen and spent the entire session baking loaves of bread to take home with them. The result was chaos in the rest of the school; the two harried staff members spent the afternoon trying to cover unsupervised areas, mediating the many fights, and so on.

Another more serious example of the overly involved parent is the one who demands too much personal attention. Elizabeth B., a Cottage parent who was struggling with marital difficulties, would spend her appointed participation days seeking to engage teachers or other parents in private conversations about her troubles. She paid almost no attention to the children; worse still, from the staff perspective, she distracted the other parents from their duties. The solution that the staff arranged was for Elizabeth to spend one hour of her weekly participation session with a "therapist"—a social-work interne who was assigned to ECE. This solution was not effective: Elizabeth continued to spend the remainder of the session in intense conversation with other parents, this time incorporating complaints about the "therapist" she had just seen. Although, as we shall see, the Parent-nurseries stand ready and willing to provide this kind of ad hoc social service to parents, the case of Elizabeth represents an unsatisfactory outcome. She did not value the service that was provided, she did not keep her part of the bargain by engaging in the children's program, and she continued to be a heavy drain on staff energies.

Most parents in the programs I observed were not so personally needful. More routinely, parents would bring trouble by making overly ambitious demands on the curriculum—demands which would require much additional work of the teachers, such as Tammy F.'s request for a sequential nature study. Or the troublesome parent might make requests which, although not difficult per se, would be found unreasonable by other parents, such as Molly R.'s demand that no stories with fantasy elements be read to the children. The troublesome parent may bring political issues to the school—such as combatting racism and sexism

—in what is seen as an obsessive way. Judy S., who had been in several Parent-nursery classes, was legendary among Bayside teachers for her continual crusades to replace the traditional nursery school fare of juice and crackers with "natural foods."

The troublesome parents are also those who, by virtue of their boundless enthusiasm, alienate other parents who are not so deeply committed to the nursery. At Park, one such enthusiast, Debby W., set off a crisis by announcing suddenly that all weekends for the next several months would be devoted to a massive beautification project, including the repainting of the entire facility. Impervious to both staff and parent coolness to the idea, she posted sign-up sheets and began badgering those who had not committed themselves, or their family members, to a work shift. The Park teachers were ultimately faced with the awkward task of restraining her, and of soothing other parents' feelings. In incidents such as these, it is usually white parents who tend to be among the most enthusiastic and blacks who tend to remain uncommitted longer, so that such situations typically set off a certain amount of racial unease in the school, making the teachers' role even more difficult. For the teachers, then, inappropriately involved parents often mean more work or more tensions to resolve between parents.

Perhaps the most fundamental reason why intensely involved parents—the stated ideal of the school—are a source of strain is that they pose a threat to the political order of the school. If parents could in fact run the school by themselves, there would be no need for teachers. While actual "take over" of the schools by parent-clients is not an issue, the activities of overachieving parents deepen the status wounds of teachers.

Faced with the continuous threat of parental encroachment upon her role, the teacher attempts to maintain a position of dominance in the classroom setting and to differentiate staff prerogatives from those of parents. There are a variety of ways in which this differentiation typically takes place. There are, of course, the structural factors—the staff is salaried, accountable to its own administrators and, ultimately, to the district; the staff, moreover, has a variety of bureaucratic responsibilities that parents know little, if anything, about. But within the individual schools, it appears that very early in the school calendar an order is successfully negotiated wherein teachers *set* tones and parents *respond* to them. Each school has its own unique way of establishing this subtle, but crucial, set of understandings (and, of course, some teachers are better than others at maintaining this order).

At both the morning and afternoon sessions at the Cottage Parent-nursery, for example, each school day would end with the teachers gathered in a final circle with the children, while the parents were expected to be in the kitchen cleaning up from the day's activities. Even in a school such as Park, where the school session did not end with such a ritual affirmation of the teacher's unique function (and where the staff was, in general, less authoritative with parents), throughout the day one could see indications of teachers "calling the shots," directing parents to certain areas of the school, deciding when it was time to move from outdoors to indoors, and so on.

This system of omnipresent role differentiation, throughout the school day, suggests a variation on the "official" staff ideology about parent participation. The ideal parent is still apparently a very energetic participant, but she is also one who tacitly acknowledges the teacher's dominance. Thus, the "good" parent checks with the teacher before bringing in silk-screening materials, states a preference for certain types of snacks or books but does not make a crusade of it, or asks the teacher's advice about the handling of disputes between children. Perhaps even more characteristic of the staff's "real" version of the good parent is receptivity to the *teachers'* ideas. For example, Cynthia L., a "model" parent at Cottage, worked at home to build a terrarium for the school because "Sarah asked me to."

Differential participation rates among the parent group and varying stages of involvement for an individual parent over time are two additional factors which complicate the staff's reconciliation of ideology and practive in the matter of parent participation. In any given school, there are typically some parents who hardly come at all, some who come but are overly dependent on teachers for guidance, some who are "ideal" (in the sense described directly above), and some who are inappropriately involved. Since at the earlier stages of the school semester, more parents participate too little than too much, and since more appear to be too dependent on teachers than too independent, it is quite understandable that the organization has developed an official ideology favoring parent autonomy. But the notion of a career of parent involvement—the idea of different stages of participation—suggests an irony: as soon as the organization succeeds in transforming indifferent parents into enthusiastic ones, it finds it necessary to impose limits on their prerogatives.

PARENTS AS "STUDENTS":
A HEIGHTENING OF TENSIONS

As with classroom participation, parent participation at biweekly evening meetings is required by the Parent-nurseries' funding agreements; adult attendance at these events generates income for the program. In the parent-education segment, the client-professional tensions that are present in the children's program seem to be exacerbated and there is an even greater crisis of authority for the staff.

The parent-education requirement brings, first of all, a threat to self-confidence. Many of the classroom teachers feel themselves ill-equipped for the job of adult education. "I was trained to work with *kids*," one Bayside teacher complained. Although a staff requirement for this program involves obtaining an adult education credential, the teachers uniformly found the course work for this credential to be of little relevance to their situation. Evening meetings create anxiety for some teachers because the parents must be confronted as a group, in contrast to the regular school day, when no more than three or four parents have to be dealt with, and then usually on an individual basis. Sarah, who seemed to me to manage the task of parent education as effectively as anyone, said she "gets knots in her stomach" before evening meetings. Describing her fears of these meetings, she said, "I always get scared that one parent will verbally attack another one—it would be my job to defend her, and I just don't know if I would know how to handle it." Jane, the assistant teacher at Park, several times remarked that leadership of parents, especially at group meetings, is the most difficult part of her job; though she has a sufficient educational background to become a head teacher, she hesitates because of her reluctance to take primary responsibility in this area.

A second difficulty is that many parents refuse to take ECE's attempts at "adult education" seriously. Parents attend the evening meetings very irregularly, and this is true even of those who diligently fulfill their weekly classroom obligations. Even among those who do attend, there is a tremendous amount of skepticism about the definition of the situation as "educational." Most seem to feel, as one parent put it, that this aspect of the program is "the price you pay for the real reason you joined—getting a program for your kids." Some parents actually take offense at the suggestion that they have to be "taught" parenting, though most react with a genial indifference.

A third difficulty for the teachers is the tremendous ambiguity that persists, year after year, about what the actual content of "parent education" should be. There is virtually no stated policy in this area except for the predictable and vague exhortations that meetings should be "responsive to parent needs," "planned with parents," and so forth. Thus the teachers are faced with the task of constructing some form of "educational" program with a group that by and large defines itself, albeit goodnaturedly, as a captive audience.

Again, diversity among parents is a factor to be reckoned with. If *all* parents in a particular school expressed the same cynicism about "parent education," then the teachers could at least deal with the group on that level. In fact, for awhile at Park the parents so uniformly rejected the notion of an "educational" program that with the teachers' ready collusion, evening meetings became occasions for tie-dying, candle-making, and so on. Such an option is not feasible for most teachers—and not only because administrative expectations, vague as they are, call for something more than tie-dying. It is frequently the case that *some* parents do want a bona fide "educational" situation, though more may not. In addition, the teachers' job is complicated because for some parents, particularly the single or low-income ones, any obligation to attend an evening meeting is perceived as extraordinarily burdensome, regardless of the content of the meetings. Childcare and transportation are particular problems of this group. For some among the small group of black mothers who work full time and hire a babysitter in order to fulfill their daytime obligations, sheer exhaustion can mitigate against meaningful participation, even when they are physically present. This point was suggested most strongly to me at a Cottage meeting on "reading readiness and perceptual skills" led by a physical education specialist. Parents were asked to get on the floor and simulate "perceptual development" exercises that could be used with the children. The one parent who did not take part at all was Diana R., a file clerk, who remarked that she had come to the meeting directly from work. She remained seated in her chair all evening, did not take part in group discussion, and, at several points, fell momentarily asleep.

Even when parents agree to attend evening meetings and accept them as "educational," the staff's problems are not over, because most teachers are not prepared to teach adults. When the staff members attempt to become educators of parents, it is always possible that a parent will expose the relative ignorance of the teacher. This seemed especially a danger at Park, where most of the white parents had educational backgrounds equal to, or superior to, the teachers. An instance of such an embarrassment occurred one evening at Park, when Jane, the assistant teacher, gave a competent, but rather simple, talk on Piaget. Immediately after her presentation, Priscilla H., a highly educated Park "character" known for her long-windedness, proceeded to ask very complex questions about Piaget which Jane was unable to answer satisfactorily. Such situations often are complicated by the teachers' sensitivities to educational differences among parents (though many of the parents lack such sensitivities). Even in those situations in which they could meet highly educated parents on equal grounds, teachers hesitate to enter into complex discussions for fear it will "turn off" other parents. As whites in these programs are among the most educated, and blacks among the least, these incidents frequently take on racial significance. Priscilla H., for example, had the occasional habit, in group discussions, of taking the questions posed by black parents and restating them in more complex language. In encounters with aggressively articulate parents, teachers are thus not only facing a threat to their own professional authority, they are simultaneously dealing with another anxiety-inducing aspect of their job—the need to manage smoothly an integrated group of adults.

Individual teachers evolved different styles of coping with the ambiguous task of arranging evening meetings. Sarah's strategy on many occasions was essentially to recreate specialized parts of the children's program for the parents, and within that context, to treat the parents like children. At the above-mentioned meeting on "perceptual skills," parents were told to get on the floor and do preschooler's exercises; one meeting was devoted entirely to singing children's songs; at another meeting on "cooking with children," parents were divided into small groups and led through several cooking sequences, with Sarah gravely cautioning them not to take too much peanut butter. The teacher's rationale for this approach is that if the parents experience the program from the child's perspective, their own participation will be more focused and enjoyable. Some parents found such meetings paternalistic. Others considered them simply foolish. But for the most part, those who regularly attended the evening meetings good-naturedly agreed to enact whatever child-like activity was asked of them.

Celia and Jane at Park did not have such a distinctive style of managing the evening meetings. Theirs was a mixed strategy of relying heavily on guest speakers, of assiduously following up on any parental suggestions for program content, and of scheduling such meetings as infrequently as they could.

Though I have focused here on the difficulties posed for teachers by the evening meetings, subsequent chapters will show that such meetings could often be rewarding experiences for parents, and hence gratifying also to the teachers. The point remains, however, that this aspect of the program was not successful, by any strict definition, as an *educational* enterprise.

"Parent education" had other components in addition to the evening meetings. Two "parent conferences" per year and occasional "tutorials" were also part of it, and like the group meetings, these posed dilemmas for the staff. The conferences were held at the beginning and end of the school year with the individual parents of all the children in the Parent-nurseries. "Tutorials" referred to blocks of time, used at the head teacher's discretion, spent in home consultations with selected "1331" children or their parents or both. In both the conference and tutorial situations, there reappeared, for the teachers, the awkward task of maneuvering between making "professional judgments" and deferring to parental authority.

Most parent conferences were, according to both parties, quite low-key, pro forma affairs: the teacher and the parent would together review the standardized preschool test each child was required to take, and have a general discussion of the child's "progress." Yet when there was a significant disagreement between parent and teacher, conferences could be more tense. The following are two examples of conferences in which there was more than ordinary parent-teacher disagreement. A comparison of the two incidents reveals how much easier it is for the teacher to hold ground in matters of "educational policy" than in issues of childrearing per se.

1. At Park Parent-Nursery, Celia was faced with the anger of Annie C., a black parent who accused her and everyone else "of spoiling Kim [Annie's daughter] rotten. Every time she cries, someone here picks her up." Annie went on to castigate Celia for not using corporal punishment: "You know I told you to whip her when she acts up." Celia laughed nervously, and replied, "We can't go around whipping all the kids here every time they act up." There was more discussion of Annie's use of corporal punishment at home, and Celia mentioned the

strategy she uses with her own children: "I put them in a room and just leave them there for awhile, because I'm so afraid of my own anger, I'm afraid I'd hit them too hard." Annie pleasantly restated her own commitment to physical punishment when necessary, and the conference went on to other topics.

2. At Cottage, Sarah and Lucy were faced with a continuing struggle with Yolanda O. over the issue of her daughter's readiness for kindergarten. The child had missed the age deadline by only a few weeks, and her mother wanted the teachers to intervene and get her admitted for the next session. Yolanda insisted that her daughter, Cookie, was clearly ready "because she is very bright and can already write her name." Lucy pointed out that Cookie was socially not ready: "She can't even deal with a situation where she has to share an adult with five or six other kids. . . . What's she going to do when she has to share an adult with twenty-five or thirty kids?" The conference ended with Yolanda still insistent, but with the staff refusing to intervene.

The home tutorials carry even more possibilities of awkwardness; because only *some* parents are selected for this extra attention, teachers have to consider the effects on both those who are chosen and those who are not. The following conversation from a Bayside staff meeting shows the contradictory elements of singling out certain parents for special help.

The teachers were discussing the additional funds that the District had made available for tutorials. One immediate issue the teachers had the authority to decide is whether the funds should be spent solely on minority families or should be applied universally. Ellen, a white Parent-nursery teacher for many years, argued for universality: "We'll have sibling rivalry among parents if we only choose some; we should do it with all of them." Sylvia, the black head teacher at University, disagreed and said efforts should be concentrated on "those who need it most." She wanted to design parent-child home-study kits for "the least involved parents. The kids who seem to do the best are those whose parents are already very involved. I'm trying to get to the non-involved parents." When Ellen repeated that some parents would be offended if they were not chosen, Sylvia agreed, but said that for her, "the real problem is that some parents will resent *being* chosen." She described what happened once when she sent a child home with materials to be worked on with the parent: "She sent the kid back with the crayons and an angry note."

PARENTS AS SOCIAL SERVICE RECIPIENTS:
POSSIBILITIES FOR RECONCILIATION

A third organizational expectation about clients is that they will be receptive to the array of social services the organization can provide, both formally and informally. The provision of social services can create some awkward situations, but it does serve to bolster staff authority, and, when it is done informally, it can create close personal ties between persons within the organization.

Formally, half of the Parent-nursery program's clients are, by funding agreements, either "present, former, or potential recipients of welfare" and are, by law, required to receive a specified number of support services when enrolled in this program. These services consist largely of referrals to other agencies. While formerly ECE workers contracted with the State Department of Social Welfare to provide the stipulated social services, a new state ruling has transferred authority to educational districts to provide their own supportive services to families in these programs.[3] The transfer of authority from the state welfare system to the state educational apparatus marks another round in the long struggle between these two agencies for control of children's facilities—this time with an apparently substantial victory for the educators. Yet this changeover in authority may prove a mixed blessing in the relationships between the ECE staff and half of its client population.

This ruling, first of all, adds a new feature to the professional identity of the ECE staff—and one that is not entirely welcome. Here we have to again recall the long history of rivalry between social workers and educators in the field of childcare. As many ECE personnel see it, social workers "degrade" and "stigmatize" their clients, while educators, ideally, "work with parents and children," and interact with clients on a basis of mutual respect. And when Social Welfare and ECE shared a particular client population, ECE was able to collude with those clients and sympathize with them about the practices of social workers.

With the new ruling authorizing the Department of Education itself to provide social services, a rather ironic twist has occurred in the "moral division of labor" in childcare services.[4] The bill, on the one hand,

---

3. California A.B. 99.

4. Both the concepts of a "moral division of labor" and "dirty work" are drawn from the work of Hughes. See his essay, "Social Roles and the Division of Labor" in *The Sociological Eye*, pp. 304-310.

gives ECE and similar departments throughout the state a legitimacy they are constantly seeking, yet at the same time, these educators are forced to perform a kind of "dirty work" they formerly disdained. It is too soon to determine how significantly this ruling will affect the quality of ECE's relationship with its welfare clients. It is already clear, however, that while the teachers are not averse to performing some of the duties that social workers typically handle, the bureaucratic aspects associated with welfare work are seen as extremely awkward. For example, at a meeting to explain the implementation of the new ruling to teachers, the Bayside administrator said, quite sympathetically, "You know, you teachers are going to have to ask your parents about their *income!* How do you like that?" At the same meeting, moreover, the teachers uniformly expressed reluctance to see themselves "being turned into social workers," and kept emphasizing that many of the new duties in question were the logical responsibility of the ECE community worker.

ECE also has an "underlife" in which services are provided to clients on an informal basis. While the formal social services are mainly oriented toward making referrals, the informal services involve direct activity with clients. Although it is hard to document fully this network of activity (because arrangements are usually negotiated privately between individual teachers and parents), the activities include legal advice, medical advice (either from teachers themselves or from health professionals to whom the teachers have access), career counseling, after-school chauffering, and innumerable hours of after-school "rapping," at least some of which should be seen as "therapeutic." What is interesting about the kinds of services the teachers facilitate is their "anything goes" quality; the problems routinely dealt with by teachers go far beyond the boundaries of school-related matters. Also, while problems are initially discussed between one teacher and one parent, other resources of the school are drawn in as needed. In one extreme case, for example, a young woman who was undergoing severe marital difficulties was receiving psychiatric consultation from one parent's husband, legal advice from the husband of one teacher, was "counseled" intensively by several parents, and for a time, actually moved her two children and herself into the home of the assistant teacher.

This "underlife" is one of the most unique and integrative aspects of the Parent-nursery program. Such a system probably goes far toward explaining why so many of the parents involved—both recipients and contributors of these services—become so deeply attached to these institutions, in spite of their many complaints. It is, I would suggest, this partially hidden part of the program which leads many parents to be five-and six-year participants (depending, of course, on the number of children they have) and which causes many former participants, years after their own stint, to speak of Parent-nurseries as a "real Berkeley institution."

With a certain sociological ruthlessness, however, we should ask what implications such an informal system of social support has for the professional aspirations of ECE personnel. It could be argued that by engaging in such personalized activities—epitomized by moving a client into one's home—the ECE staff is acting in an "unprofessional" manner. As a typical discussion of "professionalism" states: "Norms covering client relations dictate that the professional be *impersonal* and *objective* (limit the relationship to the technical task at hand, avoid emotional involvement)."[5] Seen from this perspective, precisely at the moment that the organization is doing its "best" for the clients, it is sabotaging its own goal of professionalization. But whether such open-ended involvement with clients[6] connotes a simple lack of "professionalism" or, alternatively, a new professional demeanor emerging in certain human service professions, this side of the Parent-nursery effort shows how it is impossible for many ECE staff members to maintain rigid distinctions between school activities and the "personal" lives of their clients.

PARENTS IN THE COMMUNITY: CLIENTS AS COLLEAGUES

Early childhood educators are increasingly looking to their clients to help mobilize popular support for children's services. Clients are asked to lobby legislators, testify before committees, and mount demonstrations—in short, they are being asked to become political activists for childcare. This encouragement of client activism is being carried out at a time when the profession itself is undergoing a dramatic shift from pedagogic concerns to political ones, and thus the actions that are urged on clients are typically carried out *with* the professionals.[7]

5. Harold Wilensky, "The Professionalization of Everyone?," p. 140.

6. For a relevant discussion, see Mark Lefton and William R. Rosengren, "Organizations and Clients: Lateral and Longitudinal Dimensions."

7. I observed a revealing instance of the current politicization of the profession at a regional meeting of the Associate for the Education of Young Children in the fall of 1971.

Thus, an important transformation in the quality of parent-professional relationships is taking place. At the school site the professional, rather uneasily, tries to maintain a position of authority; in the political sphere the two parties are seemingly *colleagues* in a social movement.

In the Parent-nurseries, the encouragement of client political activity takes several forms. Clients are kept informed of the current status of childcare legislation, most particularly the California bills which directly affect ECE funding. Appeals are frequently made to parents to write letters to legislators concerning relevant legislation (occasionally such appeals are sent home with the children). More infrequently, but often enough to be a significant part of ECE's collective memory, busloads of parents and teachers travel to the state capitol to confront legislators directly, either by giving testimony or by staging demonstration.

Staff and clients similarly undertake joint local political activity. When there is a threat that the local district school board may curtail support—as by closing down an allegedly costly ECE facility for example—then parents and staff typically mount an intensive campaign of petitions, appearances before the school board and so forth. Potential clients—those who were refused admission to ECE programs because of lack of space—are also explicitly urged to take political action. For example, a group of mothers of two-year-olds who could not find space in ECE's one program for this age group were given administrative help in calling a meeting to confront the District with their problem.

This encouragement of client collaboration in political activity serves several functions for the profession. From the educators' viewpoint, such activity helps further the profession's aims. At the state level, several possible financial cutbacks were avoided—ostensibly due to grass-roots' efforts in local school districts. In Berkeley, there have been several occasions on which facilities were not closed and programs were not curtailed because of intensive lobbying by parents and teachers.

This political alliance has important consequences for the relationship between staff and clients. Joint participation in political activity (espe-

---

(This was the period immediately preceding the Congressional passage, and Presidential veto, of a significant childcare bill.) The first speaker at the conference said, "The time is long gone when we had the luxury to sit around here and discuss 'reading readiness'—we have to open our eyes to political realities." The rest of the conference was devoted primarily to a discussion of strategies of organizing professionals, parents, and others into childcare lobbying groups.

cially in dramatic events such as demonstrations at the capitol) can serve to create very strong bonds between staff members and clients, and a very strong identification with the aims of ECE. In fact, the strong feelings generated by mutual action on behalf of ECE serve in part to negate some of the tensions that arise between staff members and clients during the daily routines of the school. Not all parents actually take part in or enjoy political events, but for some participants this type of political activity is a high point of the entire Parent-nursery experience.

At least for some of ECE's top administrators, client political activity is increasingly construed as a formal goal of the parent-education program—quite apart from the functions it serves to further organizational aims or to create internal cohesion. Esther, the Bayside administrator, expressed her emerging view of parent education this way: ''I think the best thing we can do for these parents is to get them politicized, get them up to Sacramento and before the school board, show them how the system works.'' While such a statement is, of course, self-serving, it represents a position on parent education that is perhaps more enlightened—and ultimately more acceptable to clients —than the more traditional notion of ''helping parents become better parents.''

But what does the profession lose by encouraging its clients to engage in joint political activity? Again, if one thinks in terms of classic definitions of ''professionalism,'' these educators are acting quite ''unprofessionally'' by pleading for assistance from their clients. As with extended involvement in clients' personal lives, however, we might say that joint political activity may indicate not a lack of professionalism, but rather a new and growing trend in the behavior of certain public service professions.[8] This development will be particularly strong, moreover, in eras like the present one, in which there have been severe cutbacks in government funding of social services.

Beyond the immediate benefits to the profession itself, there are other meanings we might draw from this reliance on parents as political

8. Interestingly, even American doctors are moving toward directly mobilizing their clients for political support. This is largely a result of growing medical concern with government involvement in health care. The *San Francisco Chronicle* of March 6, 1974 (p. 1), quotes the President of the California Medical Association attacking both Health Maintenance Organization plans and federally supervised professional standards review organizations: ''The time is ripe to enlist the support of our greatest resources—our patients . . . to do battle against the very regulations and legislation that threaten to destroy the private practice of medicine.''

colleagues. As early childhood professionals have correctly perceived, parents have considerable leverage in these matters—in certain instances, more leverage than the professionals themselves. Parents, apparently, are the most legitimate source of childcare agitation in a society which is very troubled about the idea of childcare. Thus, at a Bayside staff meeting, Esther urged her staff to hold parent meetings at the actual site of school board meetings. She stressed that this would be not only interesting for the parents but also "good" for the organization. "The other night they [the board] were discussing tearing down ECE facilities—I couldn't very well have gotten up to speak —obviously *I* would be against it. But if there had been some parents there, that would have been different. I looked around, and there was not one ECE parent there. We have *got* to get those parents to board meetings."

CONCLUSION: WHO IS THE CLIENT?

I have suggested that when parents and teachers meet in classrooms, the staff feels a threat to its professional identity. This is especially true in "parent education" efforts, when parents are called upon to act as "students." Tensions are somewhat reduced—and the staff's authority bolstered—when the organization offers its clients social services. When parents can be induced to undertake political activity on behalf of childcare programs, they are eagerly welcomed by the professionals as colleagues. So there are several settings in which professionals and clients meet, with the tensions inherent in some being offset by the comradeship developed by others.

Although some of these modal client—professional interactions are more pleasant and productive than others, they all point to the problem facing the classroom-based early childhood educator: the confusion about her "real" client. She may conceive her primary client to be the child with whom she was trained to work, but she is forced by circumstances to spend a great proportion of her working time with an unanticipated, yet very real, client—the parent.

4
What Clients Want from the Professionals: White Parents

I'm not just dumping her at Park. I'm also participating. I think if I put her in an all-day thing, that would be really copping out, but I'm not. I'm a mother and I see my kids' schools as my career. . . . But it's good for her to be without me sometimes. Before she started school, we weren't getting along so well. Now it's much better.

Actually, what I'd love to do is put her in all-day childcare where I wouldn't even have to participate. But I'd be too guilty to do that, so I purposely joined a program where I'd have to participate.

These two statements, made on different occasions by the same speaker, Patty T., effectively show the range of often contradictory feelings toward professionalized childcare that were shared to some degree by many of the white parents in the study. The mention of "dumping" the child into "an all-day thing," suggests the stigma attached to daycare—that it is a way of handling unwanted children. The guilt of "copping out" on parental responsibilities is relieved by the reassuring conviction that the nursery will improve the mother-daughter relationship. Finally, and most important there is a clear admission that Patty T. would really like more time away from her children than the Parent-nursery schedule allows.

To be sure, most of the parents observed in this study did not express such conflicting feelings toward the Parent-nursery. Well over one-half of the whites observed at both Park and Cottage had participated previously with their older children; nursery school was a "normal" thing for them to do. Priscilla H., now participating with her second child, initially joined because "I researched the hell out of everything to do with childrearing, and Gesell said nursery school was a good idea." Vera J., a three-time participant, originally came to the Parent-nursery because "it was the cheapest program I could find." Most women said simply that their children "seemed ready" and the Parent-nursery was "there." Patty T.'s ambivalence notwithstanding, by enrolling their children in nursery school these women are only continuing a tradition that has been firmly entrenched in middle-class culture for years.

Yet there do seem to be differences between generations in the parents' relationship to the nursery—differences about which, in the absence of any substantial data, we can only speculate. One such difference is the current generation's refusal to see the nursery as exclusively a children's institution. The classic nursery school, we should recall, was not designed with any objective other than to provide an enrichment program for children; unlike the day nursery, or later the daycare center, the nursery school was not conceived as a mechanism for freeing mothers to engage in other activities. But although the contemporary Parent-nursery preserves the classic nursery tradition of the half-day program, the contemporary Parent-nursery *mothers* are finding this increasingly unsatisfactory. And this is where Patty T.'s feelings become germane to the others. Increasingly, white parents are coming to view the nursery as "childcare," as a vehicle which ideally permits women free time for other options—a trend chiefly developed within the Parent-nursery by those black participants who held full-time jobs. Such a shift in the meaning of the nursery, I will argue, is due in part to the climate created by the reemergence of the women's movement, which was so strongly felt in Berkeley during the late 1960s and early 1970s. At the same time, a similarly caused restlessness led these women to begin using the nursery itself more explicitly as a setting for adult-oriented activities.

A second speculation we can make about differences with previous generations—especially with the archetypal nursery school mothers of the 1950s—is that there is now a decidedly less reverent attitude toward early childhood professionals. While the benefits to children of a nursery experience are still taken seriously, there are, in Berkeley at least, signs of a certain skepticism about the professional claims of nursery-school staff members. A top ECE administrator, while discussing current problems with parent education, suggested the end of a particular era of staff-parent relationships:

> Over the years there has been a real change. When I taught in 1960, there was a real seriousness about Adult Education. People used to rely heavily on those Tuesday night meetings. I used to knock myself out preparing for them. These were highly literate upper middle-class women who took the whole thing very seriously. Today this just doesn't work anymore. People have different expectations of how to learn things. . . . The only evening thing we have that works are regular potlucks—people come to those because they can bring their families with them.

This chapter will show that the white parents, as a client group, were a mixed blessing to ECE in Berkeley. Their program expectations did not significantly differ from those of the staff. They conscientiously, and sometimes enthusiastically, fulfilled participation requirements. The one major problem presented by this otherwise ideal clientele was that they did not acknowledge the existence of any unique role played by the nursery staff.

The plan of this chapter and the next one will be first to outline the parents' reactions to the children's portion of the program, and then to describe the experience of adult participation.

IDEAL IMAGES OF CHILDREN: THE CHILD AS TOURIST

Perhaps the best way to consider what kind of children's program these white parents want is to explore briefly their conception of the ideal child. The composite image of the ideal child that emerges from observing these parents is the child as tourist. The first demand on the three-to-four-year-old child—as on the tourist—is that he be psychologically fit to leave his home and venture into new territory. Once there, he should be able to mix competently with new acquaintances, enjoy participation in new activities—and, of course, be appreciative of new and different cultures. Moreover, the child is an individualistic aristocratic voyager, not a lowly "group plan" tourist. He *should pursue his own interests at his own pace;* he should *not,* like the member of guided-tour group, hurry or be hurried from place to place, or event to event, against his will. This notion of the child as tourist, and the implications it has for designing a preschool program, will be developed by looking at the most important dimension along which white parents assess their children: the child's social capabilities. We will also explore parental views of two other relevant aspects of the young child: emotional integrity and intellectual readiness.

Social Capabilities

The child's capacity, at this age, to detach himself from his parent is the most important social ability. "Independence" is a standard nursery-school goal about which, theoretically, parents and teachers are in unanimous agreement; the child comes to nursery school to "learn to get along without his mother." Thus, children who still showed difficulty leaving their mothers after several weeks in school were discussed by parents and teachers as "problems"—and this in a district which is more sensitive than most to the undesirable aspects of "labeling" children in any way. Of course, as Durkheim long ago pointed out, it is this very recognition that children are "social" that gives educational institutions their legitimacy,[1] and one might argue that parents who voluntarily enroll their children in schools before they reach the legally required age thereby accept this principle more thoroughly than others who hold onto their children as long as possible. Nevertheless, this confrontation with the notion of very young children as "social"—with the concomitant imperative of breaking the child's bonds with the parent—poses difficulties for some nursery-school parents. Some exhibit their ambivalence about this social weaning process by accompanying their child to school *every* day, instead of the required one day per week. A few enroll their children in the program at the beginning of the term but then withdraw them when the child's emerging independence becomes too painful. The overwhelming majority of parents in the program I observed, however, managed to accept their child's new status without trauma; the ambivalence they felt was typically expressed in humorous accounts of the "difficult first days." One such account was given by Gerri C., a mother of three, who describes the first day she left her youngest son at the nursery: "I kept

1. Emile Durkheim, *Education and Sociology,* pp. 61-91.

waiting for him to cry—but the little brat didn't cry! *I* was ready to cry; my baby had left home! Five times I said to him, 'Barry, I'm leaving!' Finally he looked up and said, 'Bye, Ma.' "

Once the parents accept the principle of an independent school life for their child, they are eager for the child to demonstrate the capacity to forge new social ties. This includes relationships with other adults as well as with peers. Many parents spoke with great satisfaction of the strong attachment of their child to a teacher. In interviews, they consistently referred to the "warmth" that the teachers showed toward their children, and some even invoked the imagery of the family: "I feel it's almost as if we had another relative, our daughter loves Lucy so much." When I asked parents about jealousy or competition between teacher and mother, one parent answered: "Well, there may be some of these feelings, especially at the beginning. But I think it's just great that there's another adult in her life that Martha loves so much, and who in turn cares for her. I'm not going to be with her all her life, let alone her school years—so I'm glad she's learning to trust other adults. I just hope she has other teachers she likes so much."

Parents are also eager that their children form relationships with peers, of course. A desire for a peer situation, we have already noted, was given by nearly all white parents as their primary reason for seeking a nursery school. "There was no one around the house but me, her, and the baby. Who was she supposed to play with?" For these parents, however, it is not enough that their children be given interactional opportunities; they should also be learning social skills. At an evening meeting at Park, early in the school year, parents listed their goals for their children: "Learn to deal with anger—their own and others'; learn to respect the other children; controlling their emotions; learn to trust other adults; learn to share; independence."

These desired skills are consistent with the orientation of the traditional middle-class nursery school. Seeley's observations of twenty years ago on the expectations of suburban parents about nursery school still apply in some ways to the contemporary Berkeley situation: "In the name of cooperation he is expected to learn to control his aggressive impulses. The nursery school is the first agency which impresses upon the child these cardinal middle-class demands. . . . The overriding concern . . . is with skills in human relations, and these will be exhibited in 'cooperative play' under firm but amiable leadership."[2]

2. John Seeley *et al.*, *Crestwood Heights: A Study of the Culture of Suburban Life*, pp. 90-93.

Although middle-class goals for the social behavior of children have not changed greatly, there is now less agreement on how to *inculcate* these social skills. One continuing point of disagreement, for example, is on exactly how "firm" teacher leadership should be. The school's white "hip" minority is in the forefront of conflicts over the role of adult leadership in transmitting these skills, but many of the middle-class parents are also deeply confused about this issue.

The child who has learned to leave his mother and to form new relationships is also presumably ready—to continue with the tourist metaphor—to see the world. Thus another element in the parent's conception of the three-year-old's social capacities is receptivity to new experiences. The child of this age should be busy confronting phenomena he has not seen or understood before; he should be meeting and talking with firemen, going on bus rides around the city, visiting a racetrack or picking figs in someone's backyard.[3] For these liberal Berkeley parents, exposure to persons of other races and cultures is an especially important goal. "I want my child to know and respect minority kids" is a sentiment commonly voiced by whites on all occasions when parents meet to discuss nursery school objectives.

Finally, we can add parenthetically that the three-or four-year-old is in a sense the ideal tourist for middle-class parents. Unlike his older brothers or sisters who have also been encouraged to develop their curiosity, the preschooler—even when exposed to other appealing lifestyles—cannot effectively "drop out" or go "native." The young child who has visited a commune which keeps a goat in the backyard, or has spent the night at a house where children are allowed to stay up late, may wish to live differently but there is little he can do about it. The fourteen-year-old, on the other hand, can and does alter his own lifestyle.

Emotional Integrity

Parental concern with emotional integrity implies that the parents recognize the child's "wholeness" as a person. The child, like the adult, has *feelings* and must be treated accordingly. Emotional integrity suggests, moreover, that the child is capable of internal regulation. But parents do not see the child as emotionally identical to the adult; the

3. It is interesting to note that what is considered by white parents to be an exotic experience for the children—visiting a racetrack for example—is often routine behavior for many of the black children in the school.

child is far more fragile, with a sense of self that is in need of constant reaffirmation. "First of all, I want my child to feel good about himself" is the standard parent comment when emotional goals for children are discussed.

The notion of "freedom" is of central importance in understanding these parents' views of their children's emotional lives. Because the child is capable of self-regulation, he should be relatively free to determine the course of his own activity. He should be free to develop new skills and to form new relationships—at his own pace.

A special aspect of "children's rights" is seen as freedom from adult authoritarianism. Because the emotional apparatus of children is precarious, they are considered to be uniquely vulnerable to stronger egos. This means, in practice, that the feelings of children should be protected from adult insensitivities. Priscilla H. said admiringly of her child's teacher, "What I really love about Celia is that she never puts the kids down." For some parents, especially the white "hip" ones, this endorsement of children's autonomy also implies that the activities of children should be removed as far as practicable from adult interference. As the "hip" parents frequently put it, "Adults shouldn't always be laying their own trips on their kids."

The final point about "emotional integrity" is that, as with so many other aspects of their children, the parents do not seem to have a fixed notion of whether their child is meeting the "norm," or indeed what the norm is. But unlike other aspects of childrearing—where the assumption is that someplace, someone *does* know the "facts" of the matter —in this case the parents are content to remain at a consciously ideological level. The middle-class parents, and especially the "hip" parents, are well aware that other people have different conceptions of children's emotional make-up, and thus treat children differently. These parents, however, feel that they are doing the right thing for *their* children. Emotional integrity is not an area in which some parents will readily compromise.

Intellectual Readiness

The third dimension along which expectations for the preschooler are generated is his state of "intellectual readiness." Here the general feeling among parents is that the three-and four-year-olds are ready for extraordinary leaps forward in their cognitive growth. This perception of the child's cognitive abilities is very openended, ranging from assimilation of a greatly enriched vocabulary, to understanding of spatial relationships, to a grasp of such concepts as birth and death. The unifying principle in this seemingly endless array of cognitive skills within the child's reach is the conducive environment: the child will reach his potential only if there is the proper amount of stimulation.

The white parent group has clearly been affected, to varying degrees, by the recent outpourings of "early learning" advocates, those psychologists and educators who argue that the early childhood years are of crucial significance for later intellectual development. But whatever lessons they may draw from the theories of the "cognitivists," the middle-class and "hip" parents I observed were clearly not ready to push for early instruction in traditional academic subjects, such as reading and writing. Their attitude toward such instruction ranged from indifference ("Why bother with that stuff here? If she's really interested, she'll pick it up from *Sesame Street* anyway") to hostility ("This is my kid's last chance to play. He shouldn't be hassled with that kind of thing now"). Here a subtle but important distinction is implicitly made by parents: they do not object to their child *knowing* basic academic skills, but they do not want *teaching* of these skills to begin too early.

Though traditional academic instruction is repudiated, the question of the appropriate intellectual agenda for preschoolers remains problematic. The typical parent, by her own admission, has little conception of what her three-or four-year-old "should" know. She has no way of knowing whether or not her child is at a "normal" stage of development. (As Randy A. cheerfully admitted, "I like coming here and seeing the other kids—that way I know if mine are stupid or not.") Furthermore, this group's indifference to rudimentary academic skills should not lead one to believe that they are indifferent to their children's later school success. But a child's ability to read or write simple words is not seen by this group as an adequate indicator of the child's subsequent success. Therefore, the question of the preschooler's intellectual capabilities—a subject which produces new findings and new experts daily[4]— is perhaps the one thing about the child which the parents themselves are most confused about. This confusion is one of the few cracks in the parental armor against nursery-school professionalism, and it gives the ECE staff a rare opportunity to offer their expertise to a grateful clientele.

4. Ann Cook and Herbert Mack, "Business in Education: The Discovery Center Hustle."

PROGRAM EXPECTATIONS

This special image of children leads to a particular set of expectations about the proper childcare program. Such a program, ideally, must take into account the unique social, emotional, and intellectual qualities of the young child. In practice, however, some of these parental expectations conflict with the staff's own agenda for the nursery. Whereas most of the white parents' requirements serve to minimize staff claims of authority and expertise, a few others do serve to enhance them.

Social Activities

Parents and teachers show a very high degree of agreement about the content of "social" activities. As we have noted, both share the goal of initially loosening the ties between the child and his parent; both believe that ideally the child should interact well with peers and adults; both endorse the concept of field trips to enrich the child experientially. Both parents and staff have similar orientations toward increasing the children's sensitivity toward other races and cultures.

In this case, therefore, the conflict between parent and teacher is not over what should be done, but rather who is needed to do it. The adult role in the kinds of activities we call "social" is typically to supervise, transport, interpret, and occasionally intervene; the adult behaviors called forth are not necessarily ones that mystify the role of the teacher. For some parents, "watching kids play," or "taking them on a trip" is something that any adult can do. Francie S., a participant at Park, explained to me her decision to go back to school and get an early childhood credential: "I used to think being a nursery school teacher was really difficult—now I see what it's like, and since I do all they do anyway, I might as well get paid for it!"

There are, of course, individual variations among the parents, with some feeling more at ease in a large group of children (and adults) than others. Those less confident about their own abilities, needless to say, tend to admire more the teachers' skills with children. Thus, in the area of social curriculum, the teachers' successful self-presentation as experts is subject to constant empirical verification. If a teacher consistently shows extraordinary abilities to break up fights, to get children quiet, to explain why racial slurs are wrong, to get non-verbal children to speak—then parents will come to concede that she is a better handler of children than they are. The following example of such teacher virtuosity occurred one day at Cottage.

Robbie, a little boy who had been extremely difficult all morning, ran up to Sarah, struck her with his fists, and screamed, "I hate you, Sarah!" Sarah calmly took his hands in hers, and replies, "You haven't been feeling good about me, have you, Robbie? Let's talk about it." The two talked for a few moments quietly and then went off together to the playground. After they left, two parents who witnessed the incident gave their reactions. One said, "She's incredible . . . I could never have the patience." The other admiringly agreed: "That little Robbie is a devil—I couldn't have done what she did."

Emotional Integrity

Parental expectations about the child's emotional integrity contain more intense possibilities of conflict with teachers. What these expectations imply for the program is not the presence or absence of certain activities, but rather the maintenance of a certain tone in all facets of the school experience. The occasional disagreement between parents and teachers (and between different parents) over this proper "tone," I believe, are a major source of tension in the Parent-nursery. The structure of the school's program and the preferred disciplinary policy are both examples of issues in which this variable of "tone" takes on crucial importance.

By "structure," I mean both the way in which activity at the school is organized—the school's attempts at scheduling—and the more subtle dimension of the manner in which messages are transmitted to the children. The scheduling of events is kept quite loose and is accepted without resistance by most parents. (On occasion, some white "hip" parents at various Parent-nurseries object to the policy of a fixed time for snacks.) But the transmission of information from adult to child, or to put it another way, the *implementation* of agreed-upon activities, is far more problematic. The notion of the child's emotional rights leads to a parental abhorrence of having the child "pushed" or "pressured." Some parents say they strongly resist a "highly structured thing" because this is their preschooler's "last chance for freedom" before entrance into the public schools. Others are determined that their child *never* be subjected to a high-pressure situation. This conflict reaches its height over the emerging attempts to introduce basic skill instruction into the school curriculum—a move that is strongly urged by black parents. The vehement resistance of many white parents does not, in most cases, derive from principled opposition to children having such skills at an early age; it comes rather from the conviction that the teaching of such subjects would inevitably lead to a rigid and formal academic situation, which would destroy the traditional Parent-nursery atmosphere of "creative play." "Why don't they just do what nursery schools are *supposed* to do—be places of joy? Why get so hung up on a Program?," said Gerri C., looking, with exasperation at a public exhibit of Parent-nursery curriculum materials, most of which emphasized the emergent "cognitive" part of the program.

Interracial differences are also seen in preferred disciplinary styles. The official policy of the Parent-nursery is opposed to corporal punishment, including a parent striking her own child on the premises. The child who transgresses is typically taken aside by an adult and "talked to." Such a policy is very much in keeping with the white parents' concern for their children's emotional integrity. Inasmuch as a number of black parents in the school have expressed a preference for physical punishment, the school's official stand represents a victory for the white perspective.

A rather ironic twist to this victory, however, is the hostility toward this policy which many of the white parents privately voice. Judy S. said: "This taking a kid aside and 'talking to him' when you really want to hit him is ridiculous." Vera J. felt deep anger, not so much at the policy, as at the aura surrounding it: "One of the things I liked least about the program was the pressure on you to be the 'ideal parent'—like never hitting your own kid. . . . The whole orientation of the school was that you had to be superhuman, saints. Why couldn't we be up front at the school about how we feel—if I talked about fantasies of throwing my kid across the room, I'll bet every mother in there would say she felt the same, but at school, of course, this could never happen." Such ambivalence about physical punishment, first of all, lends support to the argument that racial and class differences on this issue may have been overstated.[5] For our present purposes, the strains of this situation not only point to an area of racial division within the school, but also reveal the extent to which some mothers of the white client-group appear to be trapped by their own ideology—the result of which is decreased satisfaction with the organization, which, in this instance, is carrying out the group's own mandate.

5. See, for example, Howard Erlanger, "Social Class and Corporal Punishment in Childrearing: A Reassessment."

Intellectual Readiness

While the white parents do not want a traditional academic program, they do not have a precise sense of what they want the program to provide in the way of intellectual stimulation. The reason for this uncertainty about particular activities stems from the more fundamental uncertainty about the preschooler's intellectual capabilities. It is the parents' general confusion about this aspect of their children that gives the staff its most significant opportunities to display professional competence. The role that teachers take in this area is, first of all, to reassure. Alice A. reported: "I was very worried at the beginning of the year because Eddie didn't know any names of colors; Celia told me not to worry, and sure enough, at the end of the year, he knew them."

Another role the teacher takes is that of interpreter to the parents of the cognitive possibilities that permeate the daily life of the school. As one mother said, "I never understood why the teacher was so excited about having the kids trace out their outlines on cardboard paper. Then she explained to me that it was to teach 'body concept.' After that, things clicked for me, and I understood what she was all about."

This interpretation process that takes place between teacher and parent does more than simply reassure the parent that the Parent-nursery is meeting the child's intellectual needs. When done effectively, the interpretation can serve to convince the parent that literally *everything that takes place in the school is purposeful*. What *seems* to the uninitiated to be merely "play" is, in fact sophisticated "developmental" activity. Thus, trampoline play becomes "motor coordination" exercise, grinding of rice becomes "conservation of matter," play with puzzles becomes training in "spatial relationships."

Those parents who are converted to the staff viewpoint develop a new respect for the staff and express more satisfaction with the organization itself. Vera J., who had been a participant for several years with quite negative feelings about her own role in the nursery, spoke in these terms about her "conversion": "I never knew what the school was about . . . It seemed a whole mishmash of things. So it was a really exciting surprise when one day I found out what the curriculum leads to—I hadn't realized the kids were learning anything. . . . I had never felt I was of value before, but all of a sudden I felt I had a valuable place in that school, I could help provide growth activities."

Not all parents, of course, are equally persuaded by the dramaturgic efforts of the staff;[6] neither are all staff members equally skilled in making these arguments. On balance, however, it is in this "intellectual" realm that the most successful staff claims to expertise are achieved. But even an impressive teacher cannot dispel the ambivalence of some parents about professionalized childrearing. Tammy F. acknowledged a certain resentment precisely because her child's teacher knew so much: "She acted as a 'translator' of the things the children said and did, she interpreted things I didn't understand, she really understood kids well . . . but, in a way, it was a putdown—she was saying that she knew my own kid better than I did."

WHAT PARTICIPATION BRINGS TO ADULTS

The requirement for client involvement has both profits and losses for the participating parents. On the positive side, participation allows the parent a sustained involvement with her child—at the very moment the child is making his first move from the home into the realm of public institutions. Participation may thus serve to comfort the mother who feels guilt about "abandoning" her preschool child or regret at losing him. Nursery-school participation also socializes parents into expecting an active relationship with their children's schools, and builds their confidence for future confrontations with school authorities who may not be so receptive to parent involvement. As Patty T. said, quite succinctly: "Being in the Parent-nursery has made me realize that I like keeping my nose in my child's education."

On the negative side, the obligations imposed by participation are often a source of irritation. Regular attendance at school sessions and evening meetings can often be difficult. Especially frustrating to many of the white parents is the perception that the black mothers' participation is not watched as closely as theirs. Participation obligations, moreover, cut into these women's precious supply of free time. It is the Parent-nursery, of course, which makes much of this time possible, but having the luxury of four free half-days usually leads one to want more. Cynthia L. described the importance of having four mornings to call her own: "The primary thing is freedom—knowing you have time you can plan for. One of the days, I take a natural foods' cooking class. One morning, I go see a counselor in San Francisco. I joined an encounter

---

6. For a discussion of "dramaturgic devices," in the sense being used here, see Erving Goffman, *The Presentation of Self in Everyday Life.*

group. The last morning, I either go to a bookstore or to the library all by myself. It's really wonderful! I've been having an 'identity crisis' of sorts for the last few years—I really need some time for myself."

Another strain, and one that applies particularly to newer participants, is the fear of public exposure as an incompetent parent. Patty T. recalled an incident, early in the school year, when her daughter "had a fit, a tantrum, she wouldn't stop crying. I was mortified in front of all those people; I couldn't stop her. Finally one of the teachers calmed her down." Alice A., now a comfortable participant with her third child, remembered feeling "uptight" the first time around: "You were always terrified your own kid would act up, or you wouldn't be able to manage any of the other kids—and everyone would think you were a lousy mother."

For many, these problems of exposure are compounded by the ambiguity that surrounds the parent-participant role. As one mother complained, "I used to come here and never know what was expected of me, the teachers were so disorganized. It was terrible." Another spoke of uncertainties about how to intervene in children's activities: "I never knew when I was overstepping my bounds." Vera J. spoke at length of her initial difficulties:

> Being there was upsetting, I didn't know how to do the job, how to settle fights, how to avoid conflicts. I just felt overwhelmed. I still have nightmares of a kid the first year . . . he was really disturbed and hostile—they used to tell me to "stay" with him. . . . That was really wrong to ask me; I didn't know how to handle him. We're given these jobs without any training. Nothing bothers me more than doing a job without training. I really take working with children seriously. The nursery school showed me you *could* damage kids. . . . It's not like they used to say, "whatever you do doesn't matter, the kid will turn out O.K."

But if the lack of teacher-directiveness was the problem for some, for others, especially the Parent-nursery "veterans," the staff made the program *too* structured and did not allow enough room for parent initiative. "I got the feeling that Sarah had a master plan in her head—she pretended she was interested in parent suggestions, but if they didn't fall in with her plans, forget it!," Liz R. said. Priscilla H. complained that Naomi, her child's former teacher at Pacific Nursery, was "too creative." "She'd bring in all her own materials, they were great materials, but they were hers, not ours. All we could do was follow her lead." Gerri C. made a similar charge against the staff at

Park: "It's a good program, but too full, perhaps too teacher-directed. If they would demand more of us parents, we'd come through."

Bonuses: Companionship, Political Outlets,
"Consciousness-Raising"

Although they had mixed feelings about participation, the white-parent group—with the exception of some in the "hip" minority—quite conscientiously met their participation obligations. The combination of a weekly classroom participation stint, periodic evening meetings, and time spent casually around the school, delivering and picking up children, meant that the Parent-nursery became a substantial factor in many of these women's lives. In fact, for some of these homebound mothers of young children, the nursery served as their only regular institutional affiliation. Thus to understand the full meaning of the Parent-nursery for these women, we have to look at the "bonuses" that came with the participation experience. While the immediate purpose of the Parent-nursery may be to provide a children's program, clearly one of its latent functions is to serve as a multipurpose institution for women who are relatively cut off from other organizational ties.

Friendship opportunities are chief among these adult participation bonuses. Virtually all respondents said that the Parent-nursery was a recruiting ground for new friendships. (Some, like Vera J., claimed they had first met all their close friends through the nursery, and the majority mentioned becoming very close with at least one or two women during the course of participation.) The fact that the participants so eagerly took advantage of this situation to form new friendships does not imply that they were deficient in other social ties. Rather, it reveals a special friendship requirement of this particular group—that is, finding other women in the same situation. While comparing her "nursery" friends with her other friends, Judy S. said: "Sure, I have friends all over Berkeley. But you don't know what it means to have nursery school mothers as friends—they live in your neighborhood, they have kids the same age as yours. Your kids play with their kids. You babysit for each other."

The Parent-nursery also provides opportunities for interracial contacts, which many of these women claim as a personal goal. As Randi B. put it: "I went to a high school that was one-third black, and had many black friends. With the way my life is now, there is no way I could be around blacks if it weren't for the school."

However, although interracial contacts are generally amiable, they do not develop into the close friendships that occur between white parents (and between blacks). Two reasons, among others, may account for this. The first is that blacks and whites typically do not live near each other, as the white parents do. Second, as one might predict, the disparity in the economic situation of blacks and whites often makes close relationships between the races awkward. Liz R., a lawyer's wife, spoke of her terminated relationship with a black woman she had met at the nursery: "At school, we participated on the same day, and had a lot of fun, you know, just laughing our heads off . . . and I started inviting her over here. But I'd have to pick her up and bring her back because she had no car. . . . And every so often, she would borrow money from me. Even though she always paid me back, it made me feel funny. It just became too awkward to continue the friendship."

Another benefit drawn from parent participation is the opportunity for political activity. The fact that parent involvement in ECE related politics dovetails nicely with the organization's needs should not obscure the fact that such activity also meets a *parental need* which this group would have difficulty fulfilling elsewhere. The following two testimonies of political involvement indicate that the experience had profound implications for the participants, which went beyond their actual interest in ECE. Gerri C., now in the program with her third child, wistfully reminisced about the "good old days at Park" when the staff and the parents (successfully) struggled together to keep the school open in the face of District plans to close it because of nearby development:

> For me, the high point of my experience in this program was when they were going to close Park down and we fought to save it. My husband was in the Army then, and we weren't friendly with Army people, so for me this was a way to get into the Berkeley community, to get involved in Berkeley politics. We all went to school board meetings together, and city council meetings; it was great. . .the nursery school was part of the Berkeley community and I wanted to be part of the Berkeley community.

Priscilla H., also a veteran of the same campaign to save Park, describes the event as a minor turning point in her life:

> When I first got to the nursery school, I was from a small town and, I guess, "uptight." Then I got involved with the "save Park" cam-

paign. . . . All my life I had trusted public officials; I had assumed
that they were acting in my interest. Then I started going to the
hearings, and planning commission meetings. I have some college
background in city planning, and I realized those guys were *not* acting
in my interest . . . so I started speaking out. I learned to trust my own
judgments. I was speaking and people were listening! You might say
that experience "radicalized" me.

Participation also allowed for a number of activities that might be
grouped under the heading of "consciousness raising." In various
ways, white parents used the nursery to try to come to terms with the
women's movement that was exploding all around them in the early
1970s. Such efforts were reflected, for example, in the formal program
goals that parents set for themselves. At a Park meeting called to discuss
objectives for the parent education sessions for the forthcoming year,
the women listed such goals as "In a marriage, being yourself—and not
part of a couple," and "Getting a night out and giving the husbands a
chance to deal with the children." I observed this second goal being
acted upon in a rather humorous fashion one evening when I went to the
home of Gerri C. to drive her to an evening meeting. Three young
children were screaming, the dog was barking, dinner dishes were still
on the table. Her husband accompanied her to the door and said wearily,
"Bye, honey, have a nice escape." The objective of developing
"selfhood" was described in a more serious vein by Liz R., the wife of
a dynamic and gregarious lawyer: "Being around here has given me
confidence to deal with people I have met on my own, without Dennis.
It's really important for me to meet people away from his overwhelming
personality. Usually I feel overshadowed. Sarah pointed this out to me.
She said: 'When you talk, you don't have to refer to Dennis all the
time.' "

The heart of the Parent-nursery's ability to serve as a setting for
"consciousness-raising" is the evening meeting. Sometimes meetings
are scheduled on a relevant "women's" theme, with an invited speaker.
These occasions are generally not very successful; because parents resist
the advice of "outside experts" (a point which will be discussed
shortly) and because they are uncomfortable with "people who come to
polemicize about women's lib."

The most effective evening meetings are those that allow spontaneous
discussions initiated by parents. One evening at Park, for example,
when an invited speaker was talking on "Children and Sex Roles," she

made a passing reference to adult women's sexuality, and the course of the discussion switched dramatically. With parents taking the lead, the rest of the evening was spent on various adult-related topics, such as feelings of envy toward younger women, anger at husbands for disappearing daily into the more "important" world of work, and so forth.

On another occasion, Vera J., who with three children had participated in the nursery over a span of seven years, expressed resentment that the Parent-nursery had not always been sensitive to adult needs: "All we ever talked about at meetings was kids' rights, kids this, kids that—why didn't we ever talk about parent's rights? It was the holier-than-thou teachers, always asking me to give, give, give—not recognizing I had problems, too. I think I had kids too early, and that's what I wanted to talk about." (However, acknowledging signs of current change, she said: "Sarah is coming around. She said it was valid for me to want to go to school, and that it was O.K. for Jenny, even though she's four, to stay in the morning group, because that's when my classes are.")

Whether the evening sessions dealt explicitly with "feminist" topics or not, some women liked them simply because they were congenial gatherings of women. As Nadine N. put it, "It was a hassle to get there—either I would have to get a babysitter or my husband would have to come home from work early—but once I got there, I enjoyed it—just talking with other women was fun."

The relationship of participation to a parent's ultimate career line is another link between the Parent-nursery and "women's liberation." For some, participation can lead directly to a staff position within ECE itself. During an earlier expansion phase of ECE most new Parent-nursery staff members were recruited from parent participants. Although the BUSD is currently hiring very little, white parents are often led—on the strength of their participation experience—to obtain early childhood education credentials and seek employment elsewhere. The minimal qualifying standard for junior staff members in these programs—a permit which requires only two years of prior college attendance—means that most of the white participants can be called upon to act as substitute staff members if necessary.

Participation can have consequences for a future career other than early childhood education. Some parents turn their participation stints into tryouts for future occupations, and in some cases they build a small career base within the school itself. Nadine N., for instance, began photographing the children so much that she became the semi-official photographer for several Parent-nurseries. She sold photos to other parents, and later opened her own studio. Another parent specialized in cooking with the children, and ultimately published a cookbook for children.

PARENT EDUCATION: THE REVOLT OF THE CLIENT

"Parent education" represents, for white parents, the most ambiguously received aspect of the participation experience. On the one hand, this group expressed a tremendous eagerness to acquire knowledge —about children in general, and their own child in particular. Many, in fact, stated that "learning about my child" was the major benefit of involvement in the program. Yet on the other hand, ECE's attempt at formal parent education is one of the most tenuous aspects of the Parent-nursery program. In this section, I will discuss this seeming contradiction.

There are many opportunities for parents to learn about children in the course of the participation experience. They can do so during the course of a school session by observing the children at play; they can have conversations with teachers and other parents during school, or after school. And when they wish, parents can arrange for an individual conference with a teacher to discuss a particular problem. The school's chief formal mechanism for parent education is the twice-monthly evening discussion group. Given these parents' admitted need for reassurance and shared knowledge about childrearing, it is, at first glance, quite puzzling to note that some parents said the evening meetings had no value at all. "Parent education is a joke," Judy S. reported; "they have those meetings because that's how the District pays for our program." Yet further statements by the parents in the course of interviews, and my own observations at these meetings, suggest that they are often lively and stimulating occasions—and obviously of use to the participants. Why, then, this hostility to "parent education?"

We have already mentioned one source of parent frustration: some parents want to turn the meetings into adult-centered discussions. The contradiction further diminishes when we consider that two types of "learning" are typically offered at evening meetings: one is the more formal, usually taking the form of presentations by teachers or outside "experts"; the other, which is more informal, consists of interchange between parents. The most discomfort is shown at presentations by outside speakers. This is especially true of speakers with a "polemical" message—those, for example, who urge a particular mode of non-sexist or non-racist childrearing on the audience. "I'll match my knowledge of my own two-year-old with your sociological insights any day!," one woman angrily blurted out to a visitor who was discussing children's conceptions of race.

But even though "experts" can arouse discomfort, if not hostility, the opportunity to share experiences with other parents at these meetings is seized upon eagerly. An evening meeting on sex education at Cottage Parent-nursery provided the following ideal model of an exchange between colleagues.

The speaker from Planned Parenthood, a psychiatric social worker, was listened to politely. There was little interchange between her and the parents. At one point, Suzette N. said she "would like to raise a problem." She suspected that her daughter, age four, had seen her husband and her having intercourse. Suzette said she was very upset and didn't know what to do next. A brief statement by the speaker went by unnoticed, but immediately afterward, the parent group went to work on solving this problem. The group, led by Vera J., mapped out a strategy to (1) determine if the child had, in fact, seen the parents during intercourse, and, (2) explain to the child about adult sexual behavior, whether or not she had actually witnessed the act. Vera J. told of a similar dilemma she had had with her daughters and how Sarah (the teacher) had helped her. The group decided that Suzette N. should report back to them on how the discussion with her child went. The rest of the evening was spent on various parents' accounts of instructing children about sex. Toward the very end, Kim C. (who was Chinese) very haltingly brought up the subject of her son's masturbation. It was clearly very embarrassing for her to be speaking on this subject, an embarrasment compounded by her poor English. It seemed a tribute to the "group life" that had been created at the meeting that she broke her usual pattern of silence.

The parents' anti-expert bias often extends to teachers as well. It is true that the parents' deep wish for reassurance and information about the child is often the source of a strong bond developing between them and the teacher. In some cases, the teacher can take on a role somewhat akin to that of the family doctor—it becomes legitimate to consult her about *anything*. But though such bonds could—and did—develop in individual cases, in the context of group meetings the parents were

reluctant to take nursery teachers seriously as "adult educators."[7]
"Those teachers are great with kids, but not too good with adults," was
a common observation of parents at both Park and Cottage.

What does this parental repudiation of formal "parent education"
imply? Why, especially, is one particular form of parent education
—presentations by outside speakers at meetings—discomforting for
some parents? (It is interesting to note that when teachers dispense
advice casually, during the course of the school session, parents do not
act threatened; more often than not, they seem appreciative.)

There are several possible explanations for parental resistance to a
certain style of formal parent education. One may be that a strain
develops between parents and schoolteachers when the parents are
better educated and of a higher social class, as was particularly the case
at Park Parent-nursery.[8] Such parents are typically the most resistant to
teachers' claims to authority in child-related matters. Another explanation may be that these ECE parents are part of a more general "client
revolt" that is currently receiving much attention.[9] Like social service
consumers in other settings, these nursery parents appear to be demys-
tifying the professional contribution and seeking more direct participation themselves.

A third explanation, partly derived from the second, may be that we
are seeing a specific "backlash" of parents against childrearing authorities. After several generations of domination by experts, most
notably Dr. Benjamin Spock, there are signs of a middle-class reaction
against this hegemony. Spock himself, in his recent "recantation,"

7. Perhaps another way to indicate the difficulties of these nursery teachers in
commanding "professional respect" is to suggest how distinctly *different* ECE staff-
parent encounters are from the professional-client relations described by Robert Merton
and Elinor Barber in "Sociological Ambivalence." Speaking of the "magnified" quality
that clients bring to these relationships, the authors say: "Emotions of hate and love
become focused on the professional, and, by generalization, on the profession at large.
. . . The client develops exaggerated hopes and fears" (p. 108).

8. Howard Becker, "The Teacher in the Authority System of the Public School;" and
Waller, *The Sociology of Teaching,* pp. 36-37.

9. Marie Haug and Marvin B. Sussman, "Professional Autonomy and the Revolt of
the Client;" and Alan Gartner and Frank Riessman, *The Consumer Vanguard and the
Service Society.* As Gartner and Riessman quote Margaret Mead: "There is a questioning
all over the world, by colonized peoples, by minorities, by women, of an order of life in
which others—teachers, administrators, social workers, members of other classes and
races, and of the other sex—care for them, no matter how well-intentioned the care might
be" (p. 73).

spoke tellingly of the oppressive relationship that had been created between professionals and parents: "In the twentieth century parents have been persuaded that the only people who know for sure how children should be managed are the child psychologists, psychiatrists, teachers, social workers, and pediatricians—like myself. This is a cruel deprivation that we professionals have imposed on mothers and fathers. . . . We didn't realize until it was too late, how our know-it-all attitude was undermining the self-confidence of parents."[10]

PARTICIPATION AS OCCUPATION

But this parent-group's discomfort with "experts" did not seem to weaken their ties to the Parent-nursery; their commitment to remain involved at this level of their children's schooling was not diminished. Thus, when we reflect upon the relationship of white parents to ECE, an interesting contradiction emerges. What is generally offered as one of the chief rationales for professional childcare—the temporary freeing of parents from childcare responsibilities—seems in this case to have been subverted. Enrollment in this program did not greatly lessen the absorption of parents in their children. My argument throughout this work has been that such a contradictory situation arises because of a widespread ambivalence about the very idea of out-of-home childcare. Legislative reluctance to fund programs without a strong parent participation component, and parents' own conflicts about abdicating their responsibilities, have converged to make the Parent-nursery situation of "professionalized" childcare one in which non-professionals are highly visible.

For most of the white parents, impulses to remain involved in their children's schooling continued after the passage from nursery to "real" school. A major preoccupation toward the end of the Parent-nursery experience was whether or not such participation arrangements would be permitted in the new setting. In the Berkeley public schools, at the time of this study, the degree to which parents were welcomed in the classroom varied among different schools, and among different programs and teachers in the same school. Through the course of several years of observation in the Parent-nurseries, I heard the parents of the four-year-old group (those children due to move to kindergarten)

---

10. Benjamin Spock, "How Not To Bring Up a Bratty Child."

exchange strategies and speculations about their chances of obtaining a place in the "follow-through" program for the child, a special program that involved parent participation. Because the selection process for this program involved a parent interview, the parents were often quite anxious about "failing" both their children and themselves. I heard parents swap stories and rumors about the various teachers that their children might be assigned to in their new schools. The most important criterion on which each teacher was rated was whether she was "good on parent participation."

Two anecdotes, drawn from field notes, will indicate the depth of the threat felt by some of these parents at the prospect of terminating their involvement with their children's schools. The first is a description by Patty T. of her daughter's first day of kindergarten:

> The first day of school, we went straight to her classroom and there was a sign saying they were out on the playground, so we went out there. . . . After a while, the teacher told the children to line up to go inside. Suddenly, it became clear that we weren't expected to go in with them. . . . The teacher said something about wanting to "get to know the kids" and that parents couldn't come into the classroom for a month . . . we were devastated! Most of us kind of hung around the playground, just in case our kids would "need" us—not that there was any way we would know if they did . . . but we just didn't feel like going home. Parents began to tell each other stories they had heard about Mrs. Chapman being really tough about parent participation.

The second is a statement made by Priscilla H. at a nursery evening meeting, which was attended by staff from the elementary schools that the children would be attending:

> One of the worst things that can happen when your child goes to kindergarten is that you lose touch with him. . . . At the parent-nursery, you're *there*, so you know what he's been doing, even on days you're not there. . . . One of the things I've been dreaming about for years is a newsletter for parents in elementary schools, just telling them what the kids are doing . . . I'd be happy to edit it and send it to people, all I would want is the teacher to call me up and fill me in on what's happening.

How can we reconcile the almost frantic desire of some of these parents to remain involved in their children's schooling with what has been said before? Are not the parents' stated wishes for more free time and their discomfort with certain aspects of participation inconsistent with the impulse to remain participants in "regular" school—a situation in which they are not obligated to participate? Perhaps there is no one way to resolve this apparent contradiction; indeed, I have argued throughout that the feelings of this parent group toward issues of childcare are inherently contradictory. But part of the explanation for this desire to extend school involvement may lie in the defensive posture many of these women understandable felt toward the women's movement. In middle-class society as a whole in the early 1970s, and perhaps in Berkeley in particular, it became increasingly less legitimate to be "just a housewife." For many, the women's movement became narrowly identified with issues of work: educated women, in particular, were expected to have careers. For some, one way out of this dilemma was to declare, as did Patty T., that "my kids' schools are my career." Participation became occupation.

Not all of the white parents, of course, rationalized school participation as a "career." Nor did all approach the issue of continued participation with the intensity of Patty or Priscilla. Some planned to continue participating, but on a casual irregular basis. This was especially true of those parents who, in part as a result of the informal "consciousness-raising" that took place within the Parent-nursery, spoke of going back to school or looking for work. However, only two white parents of the eleven I interviewed stated flatly that they were "finished" with participation.

Although we can only speculate on the various functions participation served for the parents, we can speak with more assurance about the conseqences of participation for the professionals. Early childhood educators, we have seen, are faced with the regular presence of a clientele that, in many ways, challenges or minimizes the profession's claims of expertise. The determination of many Parent-nursery mothers to continue an involvement in their children's schooling means that we can anticipate crises of authority and status among elementary school personnel similar to those now experienced by early childhood educators. This will be especially true in situations like the one in California, where the recent "Riles Plan" has paved the way for the incorporation of early childhood programs into the public schools and has called for massive parent involvement.[11] An exchange between an

---

11. On the "Riles Plan," see California State Department of Education, "The Early Childhood Education Program Proposal." The Riles Plan will be discussed again in Chapter Six.

elementary school teacher and a Parent-nursery mother, at one of the Park evening meetings, suggests the changes that are taking place in a professional-client relationship that has always been uneasy. The teacher, an "old-timer," reminisced a bit, and admitted: "There have been big changes over the years—in the old days, it used to be 'get rid of those parents as soon as you can.' " Gerri C., a Parent-nursery stalwart, added: "Another change is that we, as parents, are not so intimidated anymore by the schools."

5

What Clients Want from the Professionals: Black Parents

> I want the nursery school to be an extension of my own home—what I can't do for my kids, I want the school to do. Take reading—you have to learn the right way. You only learn it once and I want them to get it right, from the beginning. Like history, I would feel O.K. teaching them that—but not reading—that's what I want from the school.

This statement, made by a black single parent of three young children, typifies the relationship of many of the black parents in this study to the Parent-nursery. The most dramatic difference from white parents is the emphasis placed on academic instruction: unlike whites, blacks see learning to read as a desirable activity for preschoolers, and the nursery school as an appropriate place in which to learn it. The statement also conveys another subtle but important difference from white parents: by her stress on the ''right way'' to teach reading, Joyce B., the speaker, is demonstrating a belief in the *particular qualifications* of ECE personnel that was much rarer among whites.

Not that black participants approached the Parent-nursery without doubts. Black mothers also reflect the larger society's ambivalence about childcare. Lucille M., who has accompanied three children to Park and is now firmly committed to the Parent-nursery, recalls her initial embarrassment when "people in the neighborhood were calling me the 'school lady'—I was always putting someone on a bus or getting them off." Blacks, like whites, feel somewhat uneasy about the prospect of surrendering parental authority to professionals—a key difference being that, while whites primarily feel guilt about abdicating their responsibilities, blacks, as we will see, exhibit more fear that their own childrearing values will be undermined.

The black perception of the Parent-nursery as a proper setting for academic instruction runs counter to the training of a significant portion of the teachers, and also conflicts with the goals of white parents. Nonetheless, the ECE organization is gradually coming to realize how useful the demands of black parents are for them. Their request of the nursery, paraphrasing Joyce B. slightly, "to do for my kids what I can't do for them myself," first of all magnifies the authority of the teachers. Moreover, the call for basic skill instruction coincides nicely with ECE's desire to be looked upon more favorably by superiors within the Berkeley school system. Thus although the blacks have proved to be, in some ways, a troublesome client group—most notable because of their failure to fulfill participation requirements adequately—this chapter will argue that for ECE they are the most "valuable" segment of the Parent-nursery clientele—precisely because they call upon the staff to act as "professionals."

The fact that blacks, unlike whites, are *recruited* to the Parent-nursery helps contribute to their perception of the nurseries as predominantly educational institutions. This recruitment takes place because ECE chronically had an overabundance of would-be white clients and an insufficient number of blacks. Because of the demands on the organization to achieve and maintain a proper racial and economic mix in the program, ECE employs two community workers, whose duties include locating and enrolling eligible black families. The community workers receive referrals about potentially enrollable black clients from various social service agencies and from personal contacts in the community. As one of the community workers, Bessie L., described the process: "I hear about a possible family, I go to their house, explain the program to them, and enroll them right there. If necessary, I'll take them in my car to the Health Department to get their shots." From the first moment of their first contact with the Parent-nursery, therefore, black parents see suggestions of the presence of an educational bureaucracy: a BUSD representative calls on them, brings forms to be filled out, and—most important—sells the program to them on the basis of its alleged usefulness to the child. In short, while the white parent typically begins with a general desire for some form of childcare arrangement, and then seeks out and enrolls in the Parent-nursery as an acceptable option, the black parent is recruited by the organization itself and thus has a heightened awareness of its status as part of the Berkeley schools.

We can also hypothesize that black parents approached the Parent-nurseries as "schools" because that is how they wanted to see them. Many of the black parents interviewed and observed in this study made clear their belief that the so-called "preschool" years—ages three through five—actually were a proper age for some form of educational enrichment situation. Willie C., whose two daughters were at Park, spoke about a two-and-one-half-year-old boy she had taken into her home because of his mother's extended hospitalization: "Sonny's almost three now; me and his father were discussing that it's getting to be time to get him into some program."

There are various reasons why black parents apply a formal educational definition to early childhood programs. One may be found in the anguished relationship many of these parents have with public schools in general. They feel a deep bitterness because the schools have consistently failed their children, and yet they still seem to believe that schools are their chief hope for promoting their children's upward mobility[1] More specifically, however, their attitudes can be traced to the profound impact that Project Head Start and similar programs have had in the black community. While Head Start's "success" remains highly controversial, this highly visible program has apparently implanted in the community the notion that preschool-age children can, and should, be systematically prepared for their forthcoming school careers.

The black parents' emphasis on the alleged "schooling" aspect of ECE does not mean that they are indifferent to the peer situation and childcare benefits which I believe brought many of the white parents to the Parent-nursery. However, when one systematically compares the living situations of white and black clients, it becomes clear that the blacks are relatively less dependent on the organization to provide peer contact. For example, while roughly half of the twenty-five or so white

1. Many studies point to the continued belief of blacks in education as an agency of mobility. See, for example, Joyce Ladner, *Tomorrow's Tomorrow: The Black Women;* David Schultz, *Coming Up Black;* and Frank Furstenberg, *Unplanned Parenthood: The Social Consequences of Teenaged Childbearing.*

children observed at Park and Cottage were only children, just two of the black children observed had no siblings. While only two of the white families lived in large apartment-building complexes, nearly all of the more than twenty black families lived in such apartments. Thus, the higher incidence of siblings and the access to other children in the same apartment complex made a peer situation, per se, easily accessible for most of the participating blacks.

Similarly, childcare—that is, adult supervision of one's children —was, on the short-term basis, more easily obtained by most of the blacks than by whites. One important reason for this was access to kin. Of the black women observed in this study, all but two were raised in the Bay Area or came there with their families of origin. Thus, for these women, a kinship network of mothers, sisters, cousins and so forth was available for occasional childcare. The white parents in this study, to a much greater extent, were separated geographically from kin and did not have access to such a network.

An exception to this generalization was the small group of black women—about four or five at any one time—who worked full time and sent either babysitters or various kin to fulfill their participation obligations. For these parents, of course, "childcare" was a major objective; they chose the Parent-nursery, in most cases, because they were unable to obtain a place in one of ECE's all-day Children's Centers.

IMAGE OF THE IDEAL CHILD: THE CHILD AS STUDENT

As in the previous chapter, I will suggest that black parents' conception of the proper preschool program can be understood by examining their image of the ideal child. In this case, however, their very specific preconceptions of the institution's purpose make it necessary to speak of a more limited image of the child. While the white parents do not draw sharp distinctions between the at-home child and the at-school child, the black parents have already begun to think in terms of situation-appropriate behaviors for their children. Because the Parent-nursery is perceived as a school, the relevant image of the child is as a "student." Thus, in the description that I will offer of the child-student, the reader should recall that this is not the whole conception of the child; children's behaviors and attitudes that the parents feel are not permissible in ECE's Parent-nurseries would, in other contexts, be considered legitimate.

The black parents' model of the child-student conforms with the demands of the traditionally structured classroom. The main requirements of the child-student are that he be well-behaved and conscious of adult authority. The child must maintain proper classroom decorum: he must not run around too much indoors, and he must not make too much noise. He is expected to use proper language; swearing, in particular, is frowned upon. "Proper appearance" is also an attribute of the very young school-child. While white children, as a group, typically come to the nursery dressed in play clothes, many of the blacks come in dressier clothing. While there may be subcultural explanations for this emphasis on clothing, it may also indicate the parents' belief that their children really are "going to school." This relationship between clothing and the black parents' overall view of the Parent-nursery was suggested to me by Celia, the black head teacher at Park. Unlike her white colleagues, she does not attempt to convince parents to send their children to the nursery in more informal clothes. Referring to one particularly elegant dresser, Reggie, who routinely came to school in vests, matching pants, and highly polished, zippered boots, she said: "He's so proud of the clothes he wears to school, and so is his mother. I'm not going to tell her not to dress him up that way. We'll just have to figure out a way to keep him from messing up his clothes." Although attitudes are changing among some younger black parents, nudity by and large is considered highly inappropriate at the Parent-nursery.

PROGRAM EXPECTATIONS

Because of this very specific conception of the Parent-nursery program as an educational institution, black parents' expectations about the program are fairly clear-cut. First of all, they want an academic curriculum—the actual teaching of some basic skills in language and math. Next, they hope the institution will provide anticipatory socialization for the child's later schooling; they want the child to learn the role of "student." To a lesser but still substantial degree, blacks also voice a desire for more generalized "social" objectives. They believe that Parent-nursery, ideally, should help parents with the sometimes overwhelming task of childrearing. Thus Roberta C. joined the program because "Larry was acting up; he wasn't listening to me; he was getting in fights all over the neighborhood."

Historically, the Parent-nursery program has not adequately fulfilled the first two of these three objectives. Except for some "underground" teaching going on in classrooms headed by black teachers, the curriculum has never been directly linked to academic instruction. And while all ECE personnel would certainly claim that preparing the child for future schooling is a program goal, the climate of the Parent-nursery classes—characterized by freedom, spontaneity, and so forth—is in sharp contrast to the more regimented elementary classrooms that most Parent-nursery graduates have been headed for. Finally, although "social" objectives are, of course, a major priority of both ECE staff and white parents, the problem for blacks is that there is so frequently a vast difference in the interpretation and handling of "social" transgressions. Cynthia L., a white parent at Cottage, summed up nicely the gulf between many black and white parents over the "social thing": "When Larry acts unruly at times, to me he is 'developing'—to Roberta and Yolanda and some other black parents, he is just plain 'bad.' "

Black parents take specific issue both with the nursery's play-oriented curriculum and with the school's "unstructured" atmosphere. There is, however, an important difference in their reactions to each situation. The play-oriented curriculum is seen, for the most part, as a neutral factor: "Sure it's great that Cookie comes here and has a good time," said Yolanda O., "but, personally, I wouldn't mind if they tried teaching her something. I think she's ready for that." Another black wryly commented to me: "You'd think the kids would get bored here—just playing all day. They could do that at home." In short, black parents wish that academic themes would be introduced into the program, but the content of other activities is not in itself seen as dysfunctional.

The blacks' reactions to the predominantly "play" emphasis of the schools brings to mind a suggestive parallel with an earlier instance of parent resistance to educational "play": the response of workingclass Italian residents of Greenwich Village to the progressive schools of the 1920s. In spite of administrative attempts to integrate these schools through scholarships, the local residents resisted. Commenting on this, one Italian parent said: "The program of that school is suited to the children of well-to-do homes, not to our children. We send our children to school for what we cannot give them ourselves, grammar and drill. The Fifth Avenue children learn to speak well in their homes. We do not send children to school for group activity; they get plenty of that in the street. But the Fifth Avenue children are lonely. I can see how group experience is an important form of education to them."[2]

The issues raised by the Parent-nursery's atmosphere or "tone,"

2. Carolyn Ware, *Greenwich Village: 1920-1930*, p. 342.

however, evoke stronger emotions among black parents. Some of these parents feared that the nursery experience would sabotage their children's future school success. As Florence T., who subsequently withdrew her children from the program, said: "What's she [the daughter] going to think about school if all she does around here is run around? My oldest daughter was in this program and then when she went to kindergarten, she had real trouble with her teacher; she couldn't settle down." Willie C., though a Parent-nursery "faithful," said: "My older daughter's kindergarten teacher told me, 'I can always tell the Parent-nursery kids—they're the wild ones.' " Even Sandra J., one of the most enthusiastic of black clients, had similar worries about the effects of the Parent-nursery on her daughter's future school experience: "I love coming around here, and so does Lisa; but I was kind of worried about what would happen when she got to kindergarten, you know, when they wouldn't let her do whatever she liked, the way it is here . . . then Celia explained to me about the follow-through program [enriched elementary school program], so I stopped worrying, because I figured it would be the same type of thing."

As already mentioned, blacks, more than whites, pressure the nursery schools for a firmer disciplinary policy, including physical punishment. This should not be explained only in terms of cultural or class variations; the push for stricter discipline should also be taken as another indicator of the blacks' perceptions of the connection between the Parent-nursery and the children's future school career. Thus, in a parent conference, Annie C. castigated her child's teacher (also black) for not striking her child when necessary: "If you don't whip her when she is bad, she is going to think she can get away with murder next year."

Black wariness about Parent-nursery disciplinary policies is not confined to fears about future school experience. The school, especially its lax discipline, is seen as disruptive of the parent-child relationship. At a year-end meeting at Cottage, after several white parents had given rather glowing testimonies of how their children had "grown" during the previous year, Roberta C., usually silent at evening meetings, broke in: "Larry has been worse since coming here, not better. . . . Since he has been here, we have had a harder time getting along. He does things here he wouldn't dare do at home. Even when I am here, he does them; he knows I won't say anything in front of everyone else."

Especially frustrating to the black parents with special concerns about their children is the school's frequent reluctance to even admit to a problem. Diana R., at an end-of-the-year conference, was eager to discuss her son's behavior problems. The child, Russell, had gone through a very difficult period at school and at home, often hitting and biting other children and adults. This behavior was not brought up by the teacher; when it was mentioned by the parent, it was minimized by the teacher. When Diana said, "You know what really gets me—when he does something he knows is bad, and then gives this little smile," the teacher's immediate rejoinder was "That's great! It shows you he has a conscience." A similar reluctance to acknowledge "badness" took place at a meeting of the Cottage staff, the Bayside supervisor, and the ECE psychologist. Though the meeting's official purpose was to discuss "particular problem kids," all those concerned consistently minimized the extent of any problem. When the case of Russell was brought up, he was called a "pretty groovy kid" by the supervisor, and the "problem" was defined as one of a lack of communication between the child's babysitter, who regularly participated during classroom sessions, and his mother, who held a full-time job.

There are, of course, very compelling organizational reasons to minimize the extent of behavior problems among children. As a precarious organization, trying to win a secure place in the District, ECE hardly needs a reputation for being incapable of managing its three-and four-year-old charges—black ones, at that. Moreover, what actually constitutes "badness" or a "behavior problem" among young children is hardly a well-defined matter. In many instances, teachers genuinely did not agree with parents' claims of a problem. There was also a tendency among teachers—mostly white, but some black—to downplay problems among black children because of the belief that black parents often were overly harsh or unrealistically demanding of their children. While from a staff perspective there may have been good reason to minimize the extent of black behavior problems, this tendency was very upsetting to those black parents who turned to the organization for help—not denials. Curiously, then, the events surrounding the problem of black children and misbehavior suggest a complete reversal of the classic conception of school-parent conflict, in which the parent typically denies official allegations of the child's wrongdoing.

Sensitivity to racial issues is an additional program expectation of black parents. The school, ideally, should positively affirm the children's identity as blacks; teachers, moreover, should be vigilant against any intrusion of "racism" into the nursery. At Park, there was a brief crisis because of a movie that was shown to the children without a teacher preview. The film had a darkish-appearing villain, whom some of the black parents thought was "supposed to be a black man." Celia apologized profusely to the offended parents, but confessed to be still in a bind: "The parents objected to the movie—but the children loved it! Some of the black kids came over to me today and said they wanted to see it again!" Sandra J., a black parent, feels that "racial awareness" among the children is not handled intelligently: "If I were the teacher, at the beginning of the year, I would sit all the children down and explain to them that some are black and some are white, and it's fine to be different. . .but this school just lets it go until something happens. Like earlier this year, some of the white kids were on top of the shed and they told Kimberly, 'You can't come up because you're black.' The parents talked about it at an evening meeting, but we should have done it sooner."

Black vigilance about racism naturally brings a certain amount of tension into the Parent-nursery. Children's racial slurs or exclusionary play becomes not only a problem in itself, but possibly a factor that might alienate black parents with already tenuous commitments. Yet, at the same time, black concerns about race serve a useful function for the staff. Such concerns can be used as a wedge to convince parents of the necessity for a *broad* understanding of the Parent-nursery learning experience. The parent, such as Sandra J., who sees teaching of racial differences as a legitimate activity, presumably will come to see other non-academic teaching as also useful. As Sarah so often put it, "We have to show parents that everything we do here is really 'learning'—even if it doesn't always look that way."

PARENTAL DEMANDS AND PROFESSIONAL AUTHORITY

As with white parents, the black parents' program expectations have consequences for the authority problems of the ECE staff. Perhaps the most significant challenge to staff authority posed by black parents consists of the overlapping demands for an academic curriculum and firm disciplinary policy. Each of these demands represents a substantial departure from the way the Parent-nurseries have traditionally been run, especially in the period before the 1968 desegregation moves. Each demand, moreover, goes against the tradition of nursery-school practice in which many of the ECE staff members have been trained. I will reserve for the next chapter a discussion of the concessions that black parents are in the process of obtaining from ECE. At this point, it is important to emphasize that the set of services most desired by one-half of the Parent-nursery's client population runs counter to the historically evolved policies of the organization.

Yet there is one sense in which the needs of black clients actually serve to bolster staff authority. This can be seen in the mandate to provide a specific sort of children's program—that is, one run by "teachers." Caretaking, as Gans reminds us, is actually a reciprocal relationship; clients are needed by the caretakers to request services from their organization.[3] Although in the Parent-nursery situation in Berkeley, the black clients were apparently asking for a somewhat different set of services than the institution had traditionally provided, this reciprocity between client and caretaker appeared to exist much more clearly than it did for the white participants, whose demands were far more vague.

ADULT PARTICIPATION

For all parties in the Parent-nursery setting, the irregular participation rate of black parents is a "problem." It is a problem for white parents, who are irritated that black participation is not as closely monitored as their own. It is a problem for teachers, who have to maintain the morale of white parents while worrying about the income that regular participation of black parents would bring to the program. Chronic black absenteeism is also a staff problem when two teachers have to face a classroom of twenty-five preschoolers without adequate parental help. But perhaps most of all, this sensitive issue is a problem for the black parents themselves, many of whom find it difficult to participate and feel uncomfortable or even upset when they do.

Several factors contribute to the lower participation rates among black parents. A primary one is these parents' image of the Parent-nursery as a *school* for children; such a perception leads to a deemphasis on the role of parents in such a setting. Second, this group, more than the whites, faces several objective obstacles to regular participation: more younger children at home and transportation problems are chief among these. Additionally, the historical differences in actual participation requirements for each client group in ECE—in spite of the organization's efforts to obscure them—undoubtedly facilitate a lower level of black participation. Finally, one might speculate that a certain

3. Herbert Gans, *The Urban Villagers: Group and Class in the Life of Italian-Americans*, p. 143.

inadvertent paternalism on the part of the staff may have led to less rigorous enforcement of black participation. Many of the teachers believe that black children are more in need of the program than white children; they are thus reluctant to confront black parents about attendance, because this might jeopardize the continued involvement of their children. As teacher lore has it, "the kids who need the program most are the ones whose parents never show up." Similarly, it is possible that some teachers, fearing bursts of "militancy" from black parents, may avoid confronting them about participation.

But the problem of black participation goes beyond poor attendance; there is an issue of quality as well as quantity. Some white parents and staff members are angry and concerned, respectively, that blacks do not participate "fully" even when they show up as scheduled. Black parents, for their part, find participation expectations to be ill-defined, and hence confusing and frustrating. In part, the quality of the participation experience is directly related to the prior issue of quantity. In the course of my observations, I began to sense a certain vicious cycle in operation among those parents—both black and white—who participated irregularly. The difficulties such parents faced were largely due to their infrequent attendance, but their irregular participation was in itself so unrewarding that they came even less often.

Consider the experiences of a typical irregular participant. She does not become socially integrated into the group of "regulars" who also participate on her assigned day; she does not learn the names of the twenty-five or so children in the class, or form special attachments to any of them; her irregular attendance is an obstacle to forming close bonds with the staff; she does not learn to become involved in the more intricate—and more interesting—parent-run activities. My notes on Erika F., an extremely infrequent participant, show the marginality of the "irregular". "It is 10:00 A.M., Erika F. sits at the side of the room. Two other participating mothers are running a cooking project. The fourth mother on duty that day is in the doll house playing "store." Erika F. wanders over to a table where her son is cooking, looks over his work, then returns to her place. She sits there for another ten minutes or so. Sarah [the teacher]comes by, and asks E. F. to go outside and watch the children on the playground. E. F. unenthusiastically goes outside."

This incident typifies what often happens to the marginal participant. Because she is not socialized into the more complex aspects of the school, she ends up—by default—in what might be considered the lowest-status area of the school, the playground. (The notion that for many participants, especially blacks, the school is divided into status areas, with the yard being the lowest, was mentioned by several informants, including Bessie P., the community worker. When asked in what situations she was called upon to intervene between school and parent, Bessie answered: "In some cases, the black parents feel bad because they feel the teacher is always telling them to go outside—they feel the whites get to stay inside more often.")

As the school year progresses, the difficulties generated by differential rates of participation intensify. At the beginning of the school year, staff policy is to be fairly directive, and essentially to teach parents the role of participant. As time goes by, however, and substantial numbers of parents do become socialized, the teachers feel it less appropriate to supervise parent activity closely. The hesitant parent—black or white—who takes longer to make the decision to get involved is thus at a distinct disadvantage. It is much harder to break into the routine of the school if it subjectively appears that everyone else has already found her place within the organization. I observed that oppressive aspects of a well-functioning parent group to the outsider spread even to some black parents who did participate regularly. Joyce B., for example, who was a very faithful participant, spoke of the difficulties she had when she came on a day other than her regularly scheduled one:

> When I came on my day, Wednesday, everything was beautiful—me and Gerri and Gretchen (white parents) had things worked out good and we got along great . . . but if I had to ever come on another day, it was really bad—I would get there and all the other parents would have all their little projects worked out, there would be art going on here, and cooking going on there, and I would feel so out of it. . . . So I started bringing a kite. If I had to come on a day other than Wednesday, I'd have my kite, and I knew there would be something for me to do.

Some black parents are uncomfortable in their participation role, however, not only because they do not *know* what to do, but also because what they *want* to do violates Parent-nursery norms. Disciplinary policy, for example, pits those black parents who favor physical punishment against white parents and teachers. Public confrontations over disciplinary styles are especially upsetting. Jackie R., a several-year veteran of the Parent-nursery program who had just become employed as a temporary community worker, told her somewhat embarrassed new colleagues of the difficulties she had felt, as a parent participant, over the issue of discipline: "The teacher had told me that the school didn't allow hitting. But my kid was acting real bad. . .so I would take him into the bathroom and hit him there and hope that nobody would see us."

Another source of the discomfort of some of the black parents becomes evident when one thinks in terms of the sociology of decorum. Ideally, adult participation in a nursery school calls forth very "childlike" behavior: the adult romps on the floor, reads stories in falsetto voices, engages in collective fantasies, and so forth. For all adults, presumably, the initial act of acting so undignified in front of other adults is very difficult, and white parents as well as blacks told me of their early feelings of embarrassment. But as students of decorum have told us, a group secure in its high status can more readily abandon normal decorum than one that is insecure.[4] Because whites, as a group, are more integrated into the Parent-nursery than blacks, the whites are better able to transcend initial feelings of awkwardness and act "childish" as the situation requires. Not surprisingly, therefore, my notes reveal the following instances of white involvement and black hesitation: at an outing to a park, a majority of white parents present played on the playground equipment with the children, while most blacks hung back; at an evening meeting on motor-skill development in children, white parents good-naturedly got on the floor and followed the speaker's instructions to simulate the movements of infants, while blacks watched from the sidelines; at a Halloween march through the neighborhood, the white parents complied with the teacher's request that they sing, while the blacks present did not. Incidents such as these are more than symptoms of a certain kind of isolation of blacks from the life of the Parent-nursery; when such incidents occur, they reinforce the outsiders' feelings of marginality. (Occasions which proved to be the striking exceptions to adult black marginality were the all-school outings at which many black parents participated together. On such occasions, usually picnics or potlucks, blacks would typically bring along other members of their families and friends, pack a tremendous amount of food, and engage in the events in a much fuller way than usual.)

4. Erving Goffman, *Encounters: Two Studies in the Sociology of Interaction.*

BLACKS AND PARENT EDUCATION

When measured by the actual volume of participation, the twice-monthly evening parent meeting is the weakest point in an already uneven record of black parent participation. One reason for this poor attendance that many blacks offered is the difficulty they have in making the necessary arrangements to come. Joyce B. described the difficulties posed by evening meetings in these terms:

> You know, the nursery school is just not designed for everybody. Like I'm a single parent and it's not designed for me. People think that I'm not as interested as other parents. It's just that I can't pay a babysitter every time I want to come to a meeting. . . . I'm sick of leaving my kids at my friends' or my mother's. . . . The white parents can just leave the kids with the daddy, because the daddy and mommy are always together . . . or they can pay a babysitter.

Not all the blacks observed in this study were single parents (nor were all the whites married). Some of the blacks were married; and others had steady male friends. However, the interviews revealed a relatively greater reluctance among blacks to ask males to babysit in order that they might attend evening meetings. Some black parents cope with the babysitting problem by bringing children to the meetings. Some manage transportation by calling on staff members for assistance. The strain between black willingness to take part in adult education and the lack of resources to do so satisfactorily was brought home to me one night at the Bayside cluster's exhibition of curricular materials. Running into Willie C., a mother of two young children and the guardian of a third, I asked her opinion of the exhibit. She replied: "There's some interesting stuff here, I wanted to take notes, maybe try some of these things at home—but the kids are in the car in their pajamas. . .I should get them home."

At evening meetings, as with daytime sessions in the classroom, even when black parents attended, they typically were not active participants. Although there was a certain variation between the parent groups of different schools, and even between different meetings of the same group, the general pattern was that a few highly verbal whites would dominate most meetings. The few blacks in attendance would typically talk with one another, and rarely speak to the group at large. Black parents, like many of the whites, would participate more actively when the discussion was limited to the parent group, and less when there was an outside speaker (a possible exception was when the evening featured a speaker on black-related subjects). Of course, some individual teaching teams were more successful than others in designing an evening program that appealed to black parents, and some blacks clearly did benefit from such programs; but the basic point about the evening meeting is that, for the majority of black adults observed, a commitment to attend such meetings could not be sustained. Because of the chronically low attendance rates, especially among blacks, the organization has begun to discuss the possibility of discontinuing evening meetings—even though they are very deeply part of the Parent-nursery tradition.

BLACK "ENTHUSIASTS":
TWO CASE STUDIES

In the attempt to portray the special difficulties felt by black parents, I may have overstated their alienation from their participation obligations. In fact, among the blacks observed, several experienced personal benefits similar to those described in the previous chapter on whites. Individual blacks, too, use the Parent-nursery as a base for finding neighborhood friends, as a political and social outlet, and as a quasi-occupational setting in which to exercise special competencies. As Joyce B. said; "I enjoyed going there. I'm not working now, except a little, part time, and being home isn't that interesting. Going to school is like, you know, a social event. . . . I never came in contact with whites before on a chatting basis . . . I enjoyed the other parents, I learned things to tell my kids I would never have thought of." But because whites as a group participate on a far more regular basis, the personal benefits received by white parents are much more discernible.

Some blacks, however—whom I will designate as converts or "enthusiasts"—change in the course of their participation careers from very marginal participants to very active ones. Two very brief case studies will illustrate what the organization considers its most dramatic triumphs in work with adults. These cases also illustrate a very basic point of difference between ECE's two client groups: black clients have need of, and use both the formal and informal social services available from ECE to a much greater extent than whites do.

Lucille M.

Lucille M. was in her late twenties and came originally from the South. She was married to a sanitation worker and had five children. Her two youngest were in Parent-nurseries, and her next oldest child, a Parent-nursery graduate, was in a kindergarten "follow-through" program in which Lucille also participated.

When she first enrolled her children in the Parent-nursery several years ago, Lucille participated irregularly. When she did come to school, she was painfully shy and would cling to her own children. Over the course of the several years of this study, her mode of self-presentation in the nursery changed dramatically. During the final period of this study, she was a regular and active participant in three different school programs, and would occasionally show up at Park, with two of her own children and two others whom she was babysitting, for extra sessions of voluntary participation. Her children's schooling in general, and Park Parent-nursery in particular, had clearly become a focal point of her emotional life. During the summer vacation, I asked her if her participation commitments had left her any free time. She said: "Free time? My free time was at nursery school. I felt good when I was doing something. . . . I felt like a human being, I felt like myself. I love my kids and love being part of what they are doing. When I wasn't there, I was home, washing, cleaning, cooking—my husband is very particular about that. . . . I hate housework, so at school, I was free."

Another indication of Lucille's conversion to the virtues of parent participation was the anger she expressed toward those parents who did not participate: "Parents that don't participate really burn me up. It means a lot to the child to have the parent participate—what's three hours a week for your child? Like Kim over there, she really feels bad that Annie [her mother] never came this year, not once. I used to say to her at the bus stop: 'Why don't you come, it'll mean a lot to Kim,' and she would say to me, 'Yeah, I'll come,' but she never did."

Like most of the other black parents observed, Lucille was eager for the school to incorporate an academic curriculum: "One day at school, Harris started to read some words, and I tell you, there were tears in my eyes." But she has also come to adopt the staff perspective on the importance of social objectives as a prelude to academic learning. "I think it's important that the children have a place of their own, and that's what school is. . . . I like it that at school they're taught to say what they want to say, to speak up for themselves." With staff encouragement and advice, Lucille has enrolled in a local community college and is working toward an early childhood education degree.

Sandra J.

Sandra J. was twenty-one, the mother of two young children, and during the course of this study she became separated from her husband, an unemployed laborer. She was a four-year veteran of the program, having started with her oldest child when he was not quite three.

Like Lucille, Sandra was for some time a very occasional and diffident participant: then, quite suddenly, she dramatically increased her involvement with the school. In her case, this new level of involvement was a direct outgrowth of trauma in her personal life. A very difficult period with her husband led her to seek a combination of psychological, legal, and financial assistance from staff members and other parents. When relations with her estranged husband threatened violence, she turned to the Parent-nursery as a literal refuge, spending her days there, and nights at the home of a staff member. Sandra was receiving welfare, but had begun planning—with the staff's encouragement—a career as a schoolbus driver.

In Sandra's case, also, increased involvement with the Parent-nursery led to an assimilation of the staff viewpoint on curriculum. "At school, I learned that a lot of the playing you do with kids is really learning. . .like when I cook now, I have Lisa in with me, and we make little games out of the things I'm doing, and she learns her numbers that way. Even making the bed is a game."

Sandra praised the nursery highly both for the difference it made for her daughter—"When she started here, Lisa wasn't talking hardly at all, now look at her!"—and for the help she received with parenting—"I learned different ways to deal with her. I learned it could be easier and different from what I had done before." Like Lucille, she intended to continue participation with her daughter's passage to elementary school. "It's a big step, her going to kindergarten. I want to be there, see how she is doing."

Brief as these sketches are, they provide enough material for us to gain insight into the types of relationships possible between ECE and its clients.[5] Each case indicates the strong emotional ties some parents

---

5. Robert Weiss, "Helping Relationships: Relationships of Clients with Physicians, Social Workers, Priests, and Others."

develop to ECE. Each also reveals how much this organization stands ready to give in the way of services and emotional support, once a client's needs have been articulated.

But these instances of extreme client involvement also indicate a more problematic dimension of ECE's response to needy clients. In such cases, the institution becomes an alternative—and sometimes opposing—force to the client's family life. Sandra, for example, became deeply immersed in the Parent-nursery after a breakdown of her marriage. Lucille's heavy physical and emotional involvement with the school, on the other hand, became a cause of tension in her marriage. Her husband made clear his resentment of the time she spent at the Parent-nursery, of the childrearing techniques to which she and the children were being exposed ("My husband doesn't like for the kids to speak up to adults the way they learn in school"), and of her plan, supported by the staff, to study child development in college. ("My husband works with this guy whose wife went to Bay College. After she got her degree, she left him. My husband is afraid the same thing will happen to him.") The experiences of both women seem to substantiate Gan's point that those in the community most drawn to helping professionals are marginal persons who are eager to change their situation.[6] The point to be made about ECE is that extensive involvement in the institution can—for better or worse—put a strain on the clients' other intimate relationships.

It is in those moments of personal crisis, when clients turn to the organization, that both the glory and the vulnerability of ECE are apparent—glory because those moments affirm the bonds of trust that clients have in the organization, vulnerability because they expose ECE's limited powers to deal with serious client problems. ECE is, after all, officially in the business of providing nursery-school education. Psychological, legal, and medical crises of adults are routine for many of ECE's clients, but the organization is not equipped to deal with them "routinely." This means that each adult crisis occurring in an individual nursery school is a new event, with little organizational precedent for handling it. The personal bonds existing between teachers and clients, and the individual staff member's willingness to "get involved," are the main determinants of the extent to which ECE enters

6. Gans, *The Urban Villagers*, p. 154.

into the lives of its adult clients. (It is probably not coincidental that the extremely involved black clients described above were in a school that was headed by a black teacher.)

But even if ECE had the bureaucratic powers to deal effectively with serious crises—as the State Department of Social Welfare does—it would still face certain dilemmas. Greater and greater immersion in the personal problems of adults draws the staff farther and farther away from its main professional goal—the education of young children. ECE's educational philosophy is that in working with young children, educators cannot maintain the traditionally rigid lines between home and school. Nevertheless, a complete absorption in "social work" with adults undoubtedly would sabotage the program's educational aspirations. Even though the staff is genuinely frustrated that they sometimes "can't really help" in times of client crisis, when the organization was granted some of the powers formerly held by the welfare establishment, ECE very ambivalently followed up on these new prerogatives. Those straining to be recognized as educators do not want to be thought of as social welfare functionaries.

Although major life crises are beyond the organization's capabilities, and would take the staff too far afield from its educational objectives, ECE staff members do excell in coping with minor client difficulties. Limited financial loans, emergency chauffering, career counseling, legal and health advice, and, above all, innumerable hours spent in quasi-therapeutic talking, are offered to clients who need these services.

WHITES, BLACKS, AND PRESCHOOLS: "LIBERATION" VS. "DEVELOPMENT"

In conclusion, though some black "enthusiasts" show a remarkable degree of integration into the Parent-nurseries, and though other blacks at various times partake of the organization's services, the fact remains that ECE has not been successful in securing adequate involvement of adult black clients. In part, this failure is rooted in factors outside the organization's control. Because of babysitting problems and transportation, some blacks objectively have more difficulty in meeting their participation obligations. Subjectively, moreover, some of the blacks experience difficulties, in the nursery and in "parent education," because they must participate with whites who are more educated, financially better off, and seemingly more at ease with the institution's various demands. A vivid illustration of how the realities of the outside world impinge on the Parent-nursery's ability to function as a successful "integrated" institution comes from Joyce B.'s discussion of interracial friendship among the nursery children. Speaking of her son's relationship with a white child, she said: "I'm happy he's friendly with white kids and goes to their houses. . . . It's a good experience for him, I guess. But when he comes home and wants to know why he has to share a bedroom with his sister, when Ricky has a room all for himself, what am I going to tell him?" Sandra J., in spite of her deep attachment to Park, was troubled by the "prejudice" of some of the white participants. "Like I overheard one mother saying that she doesn't want her child going to the afternoon class next year because Celia would be head teacher. I felt some of those parents didn't trust having a black head teacher . . . a black assistant is fine, but not a head." In spite of the many interracial friendships of her own daughter, Sandra is still dubious about the white participants' commitment to integration: "I was telling Celia, the *only* black child in this school that gets invited to white homes is Lisa—take someone like Kim, or Reggie, someone more "wild" and more like white people think most black kids are like, and no one ever invites them over." In short, though ECE itself has made genuine attempts to rid itself of "institutional racism," particularly through its staffing patterns, one obvious lesson of the Parent-nursery's difficulties with black parents' participation is simply that educational institutions, even well-intentioned ones, reflect the social relations of the society around them.

There is, however, another explanation for the different relationships that white and black parents have to ECE, one that deals more directly with the different needs each client group brings to the institution. This divergence of needs, may be clarified by borrowing from an analysis that is usually reserved for social services in a post-revolutionary society. In discussing Cuban education, Samuel Bowles speaks of the twin aims of "liberation" and "development";[7] revolutionary education should be a vehicle both for establishing new forms of social relationships and for promoting technological development. Bowles discusses the difficulties that Cubans have had in designing educational systems that fulfill both objectives. Similar problems have been re-

7. Samuel Bowles, "Education and Socialist Man in Cuba."

ported in contemporary China, as is suggested by the "red vs. expert" debates.[8]

Perhaps in contemporary childcare settings, such as Berkeley's Parent-nurseries, we are witnessing the same tension between impulses toward "liberation" and toward "development," with middle-class and "hip" whites wanting the former and upwardly mobile blacks the latter. White parents want preschools to broaden the social capacities of their children; but feeling the strains of isolation, these home-bound mothers also look to the nursery to provide a congenial setting for a variety of adult activities. Blacks, on the other hand, to a greater degree conceive of preschool programs as an agency of "development" or mobility, both for their children and for themselves. Their primary objective for their children is preparation for later school success. For themselves, black parents as a group seem less involved in the internal life of the childcare centers, and more interested in finding a link between the Parent-nursery and their own occupational status. This point is proved to some extent by those black parents who worked full time and basically used the Parent-nursery to supplement their childcare arrangements, although this technically violated Parent-nursery policy. The point is most strongly shown, however, in the increasing difficulties ECE has had in recruiting a sufficient number of black families. "Let's face it," a top administrator said, "the days of the Parent-nursery are numbered. Black parents, especially, want an all-day program, so they can work, or go to school." Blacks, moreover, look to the Parent-nursery to provide career guidance: in the two case studies of "black enthusiasts" given earlier, each was being counseled into a school-related career by staff members.

Relating these observations of a small group of women in Berkeley to national developments, we should note that the number of minority women with preschool-age children presently in the labor force is already proportionately much higher than that of white mothers with very young children.[9] The allegedly greater eagerness of non-working black mothers to find employment, and their expectations that preschool programs will help facilitate this, will have several implications for the

8. E. C. Wheelright and Bruce McFarland, *The Chinese Road to Socialism.*

9. Recent figures show that nearly half of all black women with children under six were in the labor force, compared to almost one-third of white women with children under six. Elizabeth Waldman, "Special Labor Force Report—Children of Working Mothers, March 1974."

future character of early childhood education. First, minority families will clearly be a numerically important segment of early childhood education's constituency.[10] Second, the profession will doubtless continue to be faced with minority clients' pressures to be incorporated into staff ranks.

But there are qualitative, as well as quantitative, differences in each adult client group's relationship to early childhood education. The Parent-nursery experience suggests that, while whites are willing and sometimes eager participants in preschool programs, they do not take very seriously the professional claims of early childhood educators. With blacks, I have argued, the reverse seems true.

10. Of course, not all children of working black parents will necessarily be placed in "educational" childcare. Yet, it is clear that blacks are a significant component of early childhood education's client base. Recent figures on enrollment in educationally defined preschool programs show black three- and four-year-olds participating at a higher rate (19.8 percent and 37.1 percent, respectively) than whites of the same ages (15.0 percent and 32.9 percent, respectively). Black children, moreover, are a particularly important constituency of *publicly controlled* programs. "At the pre-kindergarten level, 61.1 percent of the enrollment among Negroes was in publicly controlled programs, in contrast with 26.0 percent of the enrollment of white three- to five-year-olds." Linda Barker, "Preprimary Enrollment: October 1972."

6
Negotiations and Accommodations

Black parents want you to teach their kids to write as soon as those little fingers can hold a pencil. Until you do that, I don't see you as a priority.
Black Board Member of the Berkeley Unified School District, in discussion with ECE Administration, Fall 1971.

When I was in teacher training, we were taught to take pencils out of preschool kids' hands if we saw them writing . . . they weren't "ready" for that. Esther, Supervisor, Bayside Cluster, ECE

Black parents want the kids to read. I want—or I *used* to want—the kids to cook and get real messy.
Jake, Assistant Teacher, Pacific Parent-Nursery.

ECE is faced with various—sometimes conflicting—demands from its several constituencies. The unresolved nature of these demands, both within ECE and in other childcare organizations, suggests the usefulness of viewing professional childcare as a "profession in process."[1]

1. Rue Bucher and Anselm Strauss, "Professions in Process."

Briefly, this model suggests viewing emerging professions as clusters of different interest groups or "segments," in conflict with each other. Among the major points of conflict between these groups are questions of methodology and technique, the proper relationship to be established with clientele, the alliances to be made with neighboring professions, and the proper resolution of the practitioner-researcher split. Most fundamentally, however, the different factions of an emergent profession disagree over what constitutes the "core—the most characteristic professional act—of their professional lives."[2] The current moment in the field of professionalized children's services is characterized by such splits. One major schism, which we have discussed, is between social workers and educators, who have competing claims to define what childcare programs should be. But even among those who have made commitments to an educational version of professionalized childcare —those who call themselves "early childhood educators"—there remain very profound differences of professional orientation.

In the case of ECE, we have seen struggles over what should constitute the "core professional act" of nursery-school teachers. Historically, the dominant forces in the organization defined their task as the *affective* development of the child; currently, a new client group, in concert with some of the staff, is calling for a shift to the *cognitive* development of the child. This basic split over the content and purpose of Parent-nursery programs has ramifications for other issues which we have seen as troubling to ECE, such as parent participation, parent education, and the proper school "tone." This chapter will describe the responses ECE is making to the various demands of its client groups. I will argue that in committing itself more strongly to meeting the "academic" demands of black clients, the organization is acquiring a new identity among its various constituencies—an identity that solves some old problems, but brings some new ones.

CURRICULUM: A VICTORY FOR BLACKS

A basic finding of this study is that ECE has made a substantial accommodation to black parents' demands for a cognitively-oriented curriculum. The first, most concrete indication of this trend is simply the introduction of certain teaching activities, formerly taboo, into the Parent-nursery routine. In contrast to the situation in previous years,

2. *Ibid.,* p. 326.

starting around 1972 there was widespread evidence of basic skill instruction. Each individual nursery site became equipped with educational lotto sets and other "educational toys"; teachers or parents could be seen working with individual children or small groups on lettering and simple work formation; some locations set up "Math Centers" in specially designated areas. Examples of the children's writing, moreover, were displayed both on the walls of their own nurseries, as well as at a public exhibition of ECE materials which was housed in District headquarters. While a certain amount of "subterranean" teaching had been going on in the organization for some time (particularly in the classrooms headed by black teachers), the prominent display of children's writing, at events such as the exhibition in the spring of 1972, might be taken as the organization's public announcement of its new commitment to academic instruction.

A second strategy used by staff members to comply with the demands of black clients is to accentuate the "hidden" learning activities that flow throughout the Parent-nursery. Once again, Goffman's notion of "dramaturgic devices" becomes relevant: teachers reinterpret for parents the everyday life of the nursery and claim that activities which might appear to be merely "play," are, in fact, crucial in promoting cognitive growth. Thus, though many routine nursery activities may not *look* like "schoolwork," teachers argue that trampolining is "really" a vital part of reading readiness training, that cooking projects aid in the acquisition of mathematical concepts, and so forth.

A skeptic's immediate comment on this might be that no real curricular changes are taking place, and that what is happening is simply a *renaming* of the school's traditional activities. However, the new vocabulary of motives adopted by the teachers goes beyond its immediate function of placating black parents (and intriguing some white parents). Some staff members themselves are in the process of becoming converted to notions of "early learning" and to the possibilities inherent in everyday nursery activities to promote intellectual development. We can speculate, therefore, that their dramaturgic efforts are as much a self-directed dialogue as they are a means to pacify clients. Jake, a young pony-tailed assistant teacher—the Bayside cluster's "hippy"—mused, at a staff meeting, about his changing orientation: "Sarah thinks 3-year-olds should only be learning social skills. I'm geared toward cognitive skills, rather than social adjustment. I've been pressured by parents—black parents—that they don't care about social skills, so although I used to be heavily into the social thing, now I see it as my responsibility to push cognitive stuff. . . . I've lately been minimizing my concern about white parents. I choose activities in terms of the cognitive things they can deliver.''

But even with this increasing accommodation between teachers and black clients on the issue of the nursery as a setting for educational stimulation, there remains a serious disagreement over the appropriate forms such stimulation should take. The teachers are almost uniformly unwilling to replicate within the Parent-nursery the stereotypical notion of the elementary school classroom, with its images of fixed schedules, rote learning, defined lesson plans, and so on. On the other hand, some version of this model is precisely the image of the appropriate educational setting that some black clients hold. Thus, the conflict within ECE over the issue of "curriculum" really has two aspects: the first concerns the institution's acknowledgment of its purpose as "educational"; the second concerns the actions that teachers are willing to take to implement this "educational" goal. While the organization is approaching consensus on the first aspect, disagreement remains on the second.

Besides having their own hesitations about appropriate instructional forms, staff members are restrained from adopting the traditional classroom model by fear of the reaction such a move would draw from white parents. White parents are not hostile to the notion of "cognitive growth" occurring in the nursery; they are, however, strenuously opposed to any evidence that their children are being subjected to a "high-pressure" situation. As I have explained earlier, it is both their aversion to "rigidity" and their general confidence in their children's future school success that has made this group content with the organization's historic mission of "social development." With white parents, therefore, the staff has yet another dramaturgic task, a curious reversal of the first: just as blacks must be convinced that play activities are really learning-oriented, so whites have to be reassured that in spite of the new emphasis on learning activities, the children are actually having fun. Thus, teachers maintain to parents that children *enjoy* playing "educational lotto" and other word games and that math contests are among the most popular of all activities in the nursery. Celia, the black head teacher at Park and one of the most "academically" oriented of the Bayside staff, told how she reassured an apprehensive white parent: "I told her that as soon as Joshua walks in the door, he runs over to the math game—it's his favorite thing in the whole school."

An overall assessment of the curriculum negotiations within ECE suggests that the black parents are the "victors": the Parent-nurseries have incorporated basic skill instruction into their programs, and the teachers have accepted the principle of "early learning." But the only way to act on these such new commitments—given the staff's own assumptions about the special characteristics of young children and the strong feelings of white parents—is to develop non-traditional modes of instruction. The resolution of this dilemma which seems to be emerging within the Parent-nurseries is "learning by play." The following incident of such "learning through play" occurred spontaneously one day in the classroom headed by Sarah, a teacher reputedly hostile to the idea of a "cognitive" curriculum: Sarah very excitedly motioned me over to observe the children in the inner playroom. The children were running a "food store": some were cutting "money" out of brown paper, others were making purchases. Fumi (Japanese-American) was making signs for the food, asking Sarah, and later me, how to spell such words as "hamburger," "chicken," and so forth. I noted that Fumi could write most of the letters quite clearly. Occasionally, she asked me how to write a certain letter; I didn't write it for her, merely described how to form it, and each time she got it right. Later, Sarah was ecstatic about the whole incident, especially Fumi's writing. "The game just happened—the kids themselves started it. . .and they (meaning colleagues) call me 'social'!" When I asked if Fumi always wrote so much, Sarah replied that this was the first time she had done so. "I knew it was there, but before today, she didn't let it come out. But I knew it would happen when she was ready."

While such a compromise of "learning through play" might leave the diehards of each client group disgruntled, we can expect the majority of each client group to be satisfied—if this strategy is successfully managed. The development of innovative pedagogical techniques is never an easy matter. In the case of early childhood education, it can imploy high adult-child ratios, specialized (sometimes costly) instructional materials, a certain level of staff sophistication, and a favorable organizational climate; all of these, as we shall see, are problematic for ECE.

"TONE": A VICTORY FOR WHITES

After the issue of curriculum, the second important item to be negotiated between parent groups and staff is that of the dominant "tone" of the Parent-nursery. Black parents, it will be recalled, prefer a more formal school atmosphere with respect to discipline, structuring of activity, behaviors permitted to the children, and so forth; the preference of whites, on the other hand, is for a "looser" or more informal atmosphere. My observations suggest that in the realm of "tone," the preferences of white parents remain dominant. For example, official Parent-nursery "policy" is still against corporal punishment, the daily scheduling of activity in the nurseries is quite spontaneous and informal, and various stages of undress are allowed the children. We might thus speak of a symbolic tradeoff: black parents, in successfully pressing the school to adopt an educational curriculum, have defined the *content* of the Parent-nursery; white parents, on the other hand, have kept the upper hand in determining the interpersonal *forms* which are to be allowed. However, the extreme versions of each client group's position have been blunted in order to pacify the other group: in deference to white parents (as well as to the teachers) the nursery has not been allowed to take on the trappings of a highly structured, traditional classroom; in deference to black parents, the nursery has not become a "free school" with no formal structure and no adult authority.

Although the boundaries beyond which each group refuses to go have been clarified, and liveable arrangements accordingly worked out, it is the "middle range" issues that sometimes cause the greatest problems. By middle range issues, I mean events occurring in the nurseries for which there is seemingly no firm precedent, nor even a previously articulated position from either client group. When such events occur, they create much tension. The sporadic emergence of the question of ceremony and ritual in the nurseries is an example of such an issue. On occasion, black parents exert pressures on the staff to bring ceremonial events associated with higher levels of schooling (such as graduations and performances) into the Parent-nursery.[3] Many of the white parents in ECE programs believe that such events are inappropriate and undesirable at the nursery school level, just as they question their value at more advanced levels of schooling. The circumstances surrounding the "graduation" at Cottage Parent-nursery provide an interesting example of how the two client groups disagree on this subject, and how the staff is able to mediate skillfully between them.

Upon arriving at Cottage during the last week of the school year, I was informed that today was "graduation day." Somewhat surprised, I asked why it hadn't been mentioned beforehand. The head teacher,

3. For a similar situation of black-white disagreement over the issue of ceremony and ritual in a high school, see Clinchy, "The Boardman School."

Sarah, said the announcement had been withheld deliberately: "The black parents see their neighbors' kids graduate from Head Start with caps and gowns, and they would come here with their cameras and expect me to have done the same thing with the gowns, and the formality. The whites don't want me to do anything . . . so last year I didn't have a graduation and the black parents got mad, and the kids were confused, they didn't understand school had ended. So we are going to have a graduation—but only with those parents who are supposed to participate anyway today. And I'll send a note home with the kids today explaining we had a graduation."

The graduation itself was a casual and (from the observer's standpoint) pleasant affair. An impromptu platform was constructed out of blocks; each child was individually called forward to the "stage," and after the teacher said a few words about his or her special interests and future plans (including passage into kindergarten the following September), the child was presented with an attractive homemade diploma bearing the teachers' signatures.

When I was congratulating Sarah on the apparent effectiveness of the ceremony, especially its simplicity and non-intimidating effect on the children, Sarah replied that such a result was possible only because a large parent group had not been present. Lucy (the black assistant teacher) took exception to this, saying: "You know, for black parents, things like this are very important; it gives them . . . I don't know . . . *values.*" Sarah then replied that precisely those parents who would feel most strongly about the graduation (the blacks) would be the most likely to spoil it for their children, by fussing over their appearance, pressuring them to "do well" on stage, and so forth. Lucy said she disagreed.

When questioned further about her decision to have a graduation—in the face of likely criticism from parents, especially the blacks, who had not been informed—Sarah answered that she felt it was worth the risk, because "I feel it is educationally sound . . . the kids have to realize that the school year is over, and that next year they won't be coming here any more."

One of the most revealing aspects of this entire incident is the ultimate rationale the teacher used in her decision to proceed with this controversial event—its "educational soundness." In a situation in which everyone is, in her own way, "right"—the graduation is simultaneously meaningful to black parents, unnecessary and somewhat silly to white parents, and more relaxing for children of each race if parents are not present *en masse*—then the staff's way out of this, and similar dilemmas, is to do what seems to them "educationally appropriate." The invocation of an educational vocabulary in such situations serves a variety of purposes. Most immediately, the rationale of the event—"enrichment of the children"—is one that both adult groups find legitimate. For the staff, moreover, the educational justifications serves to reaffirm their own professional commitments as educators. Finally, in relation to a recurring theoretical concern of this study—the confusion whether the main client of ECE is the child or the adult—this appeal to "educational soundness" in the course of negotiations seems to affirm the child as the primary object of ECE's attentions.

PARENT PARTICIPATION AND
PARENT EDUCATION: A STALEMATE

Parent participation, and in particular "parent education," were the least effectively negotiated issues in the Parent-nursery. From the staff's perspective, it is crucially important that parents participate regularly. Their participation is necessary because it brings needed money into the programs, and also because parent presence in the nurseries make the teachers' job of supervising a large group of preschool children immeasurably easier. Moreover, some of the teachers are professionally committed to parent involvement, and speak of its educational benefits. The reasoning here is that an educator cannot hope to "reach" a young child who is seen only a few hours a day unless the professional is simultaneously involved with the major influence in the child's life, his parent. Finally, some staff members, troubled by the claims that parental authority is disrupted by professionalized childcare, feel "ideological" pulls toward parent involvement.

The parents' feelings about participation are somewhat more ambivalent. They too acknowledge the ideological and educational arguments for their involvement in the Parent-nursery. They also recognize that when they enroll in the program, they undertake a contractual obligation to participate. Yet, as we have seen, many parents do not fully meet their obligations. Some fine it objectively difficult to come regularly to the nurseries. Others feel "ideological" pulls *away* from participating—they feel that a preschool program is for children and should free adults for other activities. As an attempt to simplify this complex set of reactions, we might say that parents feel they should be allowed to participate, but not be obliged to do so.

ECE is dealing in two ways with parental reluctance to participate regularly. The first is to increasingly assign parents "credit hours" for tasks done outside the schools. These credit-gaining activities can be strictly limited to direct school business, such as typing school records and preparing curricular materials, or they can be interpreted more broadly to include various activities that will ultimately "benefit" the school or an individual child, such as attending community-wide childcare workshops or studying specialized writings on child development. One of many difficulties that this solution brings, however, is the intensified climate of negotiation it produces between teacher and parent, as the parent demands "credit hours" for various activities that stretch or break the boundaries of what is administratively reasonable.[4]

A second and related organizational response to uneven parent participation is simply to move toward a situation in which parent involvement is no longer required. The Parent-nurseries, both by tradition and by their present funding arrangements, are dependent on regular parent participation. Newer ECE institutions, such as the Early Learning Center, are moving toward a model of voluntary parent involvement. As ECE programs increasingly are located directly in public schools, presumably the financial reliance on parent involvement will decline or cease.

The Parent-nursery staff's inability to find a satisfactory definition of "parent education" is the most troublesome aspect of the already difficult issue of parent participation. One problem with ECE's parent education efforts is simply the breakdown of the traditional form of parent education in the nursery, the evening meeting. As one administrator said:

> In the old days, the Tuesday night meetings was sacred—that's what the Parent-nursery was all about . . . the parents loved these meetings, and so did we . . . but now we have a different population . . . some of our parents won't come out for a Tuesday night anything! So if the evening meeting isn't going to work any more, we'll have to try other things—occasional potlucks, maybe earlier in the day, with the children; meetings in the afternoon; smaller meetings, maybe not the whole parent group. I know it's hard for the Parent-nursery staff to accept, but I think the weekly evening meeting has had it.

4. This individually negotiated system of credit-hour granting also served to exacerbate racial strain among parents. Whites felt that blacks were granted these hours more readily than whites. At Cottage Parent-nursery, a teacher gave credit hours to a black parent who had read to her child at bedtime. When a white parent, who overheard this transaction, demanded similar credits, the teacher refused. The teacher argued that the white parent "always" read to her children, while for this black parent, such reading was a new experience. The white parent was very dissatisfied with the teacher's ruling.

But even with gradual staff willingness to try alternatives to the evening meeting, parent education remains a problem. There does not seem to be any agreement between staff members and parents (or among staff members themselves) as to what Parent Education should be. The models of parent education being developed elsewhere in the profession are unacceptable to many of the teachers and parents.

The classic nursery educators' position on parent education, developed in response to a middle-class clientele, is that early childhood professionals should *instruct* young mothers in ways to be better parents. Such instruction typically would take place at the school site. However, the growth in recent years of the "compensatory" segment of the profession has expanded and intensified professionals' impulses for parent education. Using the argument that a necessary precondition for helping the "culturally deprived" child is improving the childrearing techniques of the "culturally deprived" mother, some within the compensatory movement have called for concerted efforts at home-based intervention. Head Start has given birth to Home Start.

An aggressively interventionist notion of parent education, whether home or school-based, is very difficult for ECE to endorse publicly. In Berkeley, the sensitivities of both of its client groups, the liberal characteristics of the school district and the city at large, and the political sophistication of many individual staff members—all made it impossible for ECE to identify with such a "paternalistic" model. However, while it largely repudiated the interventionist approach, it was left with no coherent notion of what parent education should be. As we saw, Esther, the Bayside supervisor, suggested that a legitimate goal of parent education should be familiarization with political processes, and the encouragement of political activism in the childcare arena; another ECE administrator suggested that the organization itself should not set specific goals for parent education, but should respond to the various demands of clients in this area as they come up. At the present time, we may conclude that for staff and parents alike, parent education remains one of the least understood aspects of early childhood services.

INTERNAL NEGOTIATIONS: TEACHERS AND ADMINISTRATORS

The major accommodation that has been made to clients by ECE is the shift toward a cognitively oriented program. In this section, I will discuss how administrators and teachers are attempting to act on this new commitment. What does this shift imply for classroom practice?

How will the new focus bear on the professional aspirations of the early childhood educators? What tensions might arise between administrators and teachers as the organization moves to implement the new program?

From the administrative perspective, the development of a cognitively based curriculum for preschoolers requires that teachers acquire a new body of knowledge. The administrators' special role in this situation is to spell out for the teachers what they need to know in the face of the new mandate to offer more "academic" instruction. Like the efforts of their colleagues elsewhere in the profession,[5] the attempts of ECE leaders to construct a preschool curriculum draws heavily from recent work in cognitive psychology, and most particularly from the work of Piaget. The aspect of this work that the educators rely on most has to do with the stages of children's intellectual development. As the administrators understand it, the construction of a cognitively based curriculum is a threefold operation: first, the staff itself must become familiar with a large (and difficult) body of material; second, a classroom program must be derived from this highly abstract literature; and third, as suggested earlier, a pedagogic style must be developed that will insure learning in a "non-rigid" manner.

The hesitations of some of the teachers are a major obstacle to administrative efforts to incorporate a cognitive approach into the workings of the organization. Hughes has spoken of the difficulties that arise when an occupation is in transition, and some of the people in the occupation "are not mobile enough to go along with the changes."[6] Such a phenomenon seems to be occurring in ECE ranks. Older staff members, especially, who were trained with a particular orientation to nursery education, find it extremely difficult to be "remade" into the cognitive mold. In particular, some of the "old-timers" fear the devaluation of play and spontaneity that the new era might bring. As Esther sympathetically said: "I was trained that way myself, and I know how hard it is for them to give all those old things up. . . . I'm having a very difficult time getting some of those teachers to make the shift."

Generally speaking, in Berkeley the new cognitive thrust appeared to have more support among black teachers than among whites. In spite of variations of age and training among the black teachers, as a group they

5. See, for example, Millie Almy, "Piaget in Action," and "Spontaneous Play: An Avenue for Intellectual Development;" Ann Hammerman and Susan Morse, "Open Teaching: Piaget in the Classroom;" Bettye Caldwell, "On Designing Supplementary Environments for Early Childhood Development;" and Joe L. Frost and G. Thomas Rowland, "Curricula for the Seventies."

6. Hughes, *The Sociological Eye*, p. 340.

could be expected to be more in tune with the demands of the black parents. In several ECE Parent-nurseries, even before the deliberations over a new curriculum began, some black teachers had for some time been carrying on a quasi-covert program of basic skill instruction. In fact, one problem facing administrators is that some black teachers will embrace the new cognitive aims *too* eagerly, and break the delicate balance which the organization is trying to achieve.

But the "ideological" positions of individual teachers, either for or against the new curriculum, are not the only factor which will determine the staff's predisposition to assimilate this body of knowledge. Another factor is the circumstances under which the new material is presented, and the priority it will be given. The obvious organizational mechanism for presenting the new material would be the existing weekly in-service meeting of the staff. But teachers and administrators have different conceptions of what the priorities of in-service meetings should be. For example, during the period of my observations, Esther wanted to use in-service meetings to "turn the staff on" to cognitive theory. She prepared long discussion sessions on Piaget, and on other theorists such as Erik Erikson. The teachers, however, also want to use the meetings to discuss daily problems encountered in the nurseries. As Jane, the young assistant teacher at Park—who, in fact, was unusually skilled in constructing Piaget-derived classroom materials—told me: "Esther wants to use those meetings to talk about theories. There's nothing wrong with that per se—it's just that the teachers want to talk about why no one is coming to their evening meetings, what to do about a problem kid—we really want to find out what's happening in each other's classrooms . . . share ideas, help each other out."

The divergence between administrators and teachers as to what should be the priorities of in-service meetings provide an interesting insight into the division of labor within this organization. The administrators are engaged in the process of defining what the ECE staff as a whole "needs to know" because that is, after all, their job.[7] Furthermore, because of ECE's particular status as a showpiece organization, administrators can justifiably feel that on some level they are also defining priorities for the profession at large. Teachers, on the other hand, have an understadable interest in being given the opportunity to discuss poor adult attendance, because getting parents to participate is their job.

7. Selznick, *Leadership in Administration*.

Similarly, the division of labor within ECE makes administrators more acutely aware of the possible relation between the new cognitive emphasis and "professionalization." Both parties realize the status difficulties of ECE, and the field of early childhood education in general; each has a somewhat different notion of the solution to these problems. Teachers believe that the problem confronting ECE can be solved by an increased allocation of financial resources and more public understanding and approval of the nursery-school enterprise. Administrators have no quarrel with these objectives, but they also see the long-range necessity of *transforming the persons* who work within the organization. "I want my staff to become intellectuals," Esther said only half-jokingly. The new curriculum, of course, calls for considerable staff re-education.

There are, of course, variations in the teachers' reactions to the newly emerging curriculum. Some are offended by it, some are indifferent to it, while others—whites as well as blacks—are gradually becoming intrigued, and even enthusiastic about it. But whatever the level of individual receptivity, the dominant concern of all the teachers is to manage successfully the considerable demands of daily life in the Parent-nurseries. It is a job which is both physically and psychically demanding and one which does not, from the teachers' perspective, leave much space for them to be remade into Piagetian experts. For many teachers, then, the development of a cognitive program is still largely an accommodation to administration and clients. As one teacher sighed after the staff meeting at which Esther announced plans for the public exhibition of Bayside curricular materials: "Sure, we'll pull something together . . . but we're doing it really because she asked us to—this cognitive business is Esther's thing."

In contrast, the dominant concern of administrators, freed from direct classroom responsibilities, is the promotion of ECE programs as legitimate components of public education in Berkeley. To administrators, therefore, the new curriculum is not only viewed as a strategic concession to a valuable client group, but also as a potential mechanism for organizational upgrading.

COGNITIVE CURRICULUM:
THE NEW LEGITIMACY OF ECE

Finally, we should ask what consequences ECE's movement toward a cognitively based program has for the organization's relation to the local and state educational establishments. One historic source of ECE's marginality has been the accusation that its preschool programs were not providing "real" education; presumably, ECE's emerging emphasis on "early learning" should constitute a major step forward in securing new legitimacy.

Such an increasing acceptance of early childhood programs on the part of the BUSD is already occurring. During the course of this study, developments both within the district and outside of it converged to solidify ECE's formal place within the Berkeley schools. Central administrators began to discuss plans whereby the Parent-nurseries and other early childhood programs would be transplanted to elementary school sites.[8] The "Early Learning Center" concept, ECE's newest program effort, began to receive close attention from the BUSD administration and members of the school board. Returning to our original characterization of ECE as a "precarious organization," we might say, in light of the fact that its programs are being located directly within the elementary schools, that ECE has "arrived." It would seem to be moving out of its historic state of marginality.

ECE's rising fortunes can be attributed partly to the organization's emerging commitment to a cognitive curriculum. Here again we must recall the school district's continuing agony over the achievement gap between white and minority children. As long as ECE was not perceived by key persons to be part of the struggle to reduce this gap, there existed only a very tentative climate of support for the organization. The cool reception, quoted at the beginning of this chapter, to the ECE administration in 1971, was symptomatic of many interactions between ECE and the school board in the "precognitive era." Thus, it appears that ECE's newly "academic" self-presentation, coupled with the mounting evidence of the special possibilities of early learning for minority children,[9] has changed the organization's position considerably. We can further speculate that ECE, and programs like it elsewhere in the nation, are momentarily benefitting from the crisis in confidence facing public education as a whole; because nothing else seems to "work," especially high hopes are being fastened on preschool efforts.[10]

8. BUSD, "Buildings in Berkeley."

9. The question of which preschool programs, if any, are "successful" remains highly controversial. Among the studies which suggest some gain for the "disadvantaged" through exposure to programs, are Joan Bissell, "The Cognitive Effect of Pre-School Programs for Disadvantaged Children;" and Miriam Stearns, "Report on Pre-School Programs: The Effect of Pre-School Programs on Disadvantaged Children and Their Families." Bane, in "Open Education," suggests that structured programs are more effective for disadvantaged pre-schoolers than non-structured ones.

10. See Marvin Lazerson, "Social Reform and Early Childhood Education."

There are, however, more pragmatic reasons for the changes in the status of ECE programs. First, the Berkeley schools are faced with declining numbers of children of elementary school age.[11] Second, the BUSD, like other districts, is in a state of acknowledged financial crisis. The combination of empty classrooms and financial panic has led central district administrators to propose that various ECE programs be housed within elementary school sites. Among other advantages, this plan would have the virtue of saving the district the high maintenance cost of the presently separate ECE facilities. An additional obvious advantage this plan would bring to the host elementary school is that the new ECE children would generate "average daily attendance" monies for the school. It is impossible, of course, to determine precisely how much of the district's increased receptivity to ECE's programs stems from a new "philosophic" acceptance of early education and how much is simply a function of the economic and demographic factors just mentioned. What is important for our purposes, however, is that the probable link between preschool experience and later academic success—in combination with ECE's emerging commitments to a cognitive curriculum—offers the district its most useful educational justification for bringing early childhood programs into the elementary schools.

ECE AND THE "RILES PLAN"

These developments in Berkeley coincided with the beginnings of a statewide reorganization of California primary education led by Wilson Riles, the State Superintendent of Public Instruction.[12] The Riles Plan, which at this writing is still in the process of being implemented, has the following features: the incorporation of four-year-olds into elementary programs (on a voluntary basis); the designation of ages four through eight as the target population for a new program of "early childhood education;" an "individualized" curriculum for each child; extensive parent participation in classrooms; and new emphasis on parent education. Legislative approval for the Riles Plan was obtained in late 1972,[13] and the first phase of the plan was implemented in the fall of 1973. In the several years since its inception, the plan has attracted considerable

11. BUSD, "Buildings in Berkeley."

12. California State Department of Education, "Report of Task Force on Early Childhood Education to Superintendent Riles," and "Early Childhood Education Program Proposal."

13. California S.B. 1302.

nationwide attention (and controversy).[14] The California program is seen by some as a possible model for a national early childhood policy.

The recommendations of the Riles task force have, predictably, brought a significant boost in status for early childhood educators in California, if not nationally. The plan's affirmation of "the first eight years of life [as] the most important period in determining the future effectiveness of all our citizens,"[15] the stress on individualized curricula and parent involvement, and, especially, the recognition of four-year-olds as a logical program clientele are all, of course, part of the standard nursery educator's lexicon. Perhaps the greatest symbolic victory of all for the profession is that the state planners have adopted its name: this plan for reorganizing elementary schools is called the Early Childhood Education Program.

The Berkeley Unified School District has played an important role in these statewide developments. From the inception of the plan, individual ECE administrators were consulted by the Riles staff as various phases of the program were being developed. Most significantly, it was expected that the two Early Learning Centers, which the district operated in the early 1970s through ECE, would serve as a model for similar efforts across the state to implement the Riles proposals. In sum, then, the events surrounding the development of this new plan are serving both to highlight the BUSD's position as a leading provider of early childhood programs, and to increase the general legitimacy of preschool education in California.

Ironically, however, during the period of these converging developments at the state and local level (1971-1973), ECE's reaction to its newfound success contained elements of fear and skepticism as well as elation. The most negative reactions to these events came from classroom-based staff. The staff's fear was that transfer into elementary school settings would make *nursery* school education as they now practiced it impossible. As one teacher put it at a staff meeting: "How

14. See the *New York Times*, "California Programs Shift Funds to Youngest Pupils," February 24, 1975, pp. 1 and 50. Raymond Moore has emerged as one of the leading critics of early-learning programs in general, and of the Riles program in particular. See his "The California Report: Early Schooling for All?," and "Further Comments on the California Report," and the replies by Burton White *et al.*, "When Should Schooling Begin?;" Elizabeth Lewis, "The Real California Report: A New Approach to Education;" and Ruth Highberger and Sharon Teets, "Early Schooling: Why Not? A Reply to Raymond and Dennis Moore."

15. California State Department of Education, "Early Childhood Education Program Proposal," p. 1.

can we carry on our program when the schools run on bells, when there're forty kids in a classroom, when the principal thinks a noisy classroom means trouble, when you're not supposed to be on the playground except at recess?" Some teachers drew comparisons between their situation and that of the kindergarten movement of the nineteenth century, pointing out the virtual sabotage of the movement's pedagogical principles that occurred with the absorption of kindergartens into public schools.

These teachers were quite dubious about the Riles Plan's stated aim of "humanizing" elementary schools by bringing in both the younger children and the practices associated with early childhood education. "They say *we're* supposed to 'change *them*,' but you know *they* are going to change *us* . . . they're going to be expecting us to teach reading and writing to a large group, just like in first and second grade." Such statements point to the teachers' fear that the delicate web of negotiations which have been worked out within the Parent-nursery between clients and staff members would fall apart in the context of the elementary school. The teachers were afraid that the tradeoff of basic skill instruction (as blacks demanded) for innovative pedagogical methods and a relaxed disciplinary style (which white parents and many teachers themselves required) would become impossible. Their assumption was that principals and other teachers within the elementary school would not be able to support such deviations from standard school practice. The Parent-nursery teachers also pointed out that the elementary schools were likely to have difficulties with the parent involvement traditionally associated with nursery education. As some of the classroom teachers saw it, therefore, their "integrity" as nursery teachers was at stake.

Administrators' responses to these new developments showed the same hesitations, but also contained elements of optimism. In part, the difference stemmed from the greater opportunities for political sophistication on the part of the administrators. Being in close contact with officials of both the BUSD and the State Department of Education, administrators were more aware of the long-term inevitability of these developments, and hence were relatively more prepared to try to make the best of them. Furthermore, within limits, ECE administrators were in a better position to affect the course of things to come, both locally and to a lesser extent in the state. Classroom teachers, who did not have such direct access to higher levels of authority, were, of course, in a far more passive role. Still another way of looking at the difference in reaction between teachers and administrators is to return to the different orientation of each toward "professionalization." As with the prior issue of a cognitively based curriculum, administrators seemed to be more aware that a movement into public school settings carried with it possibilities of upward mobility for early childhood education. This is not to suggest that various ECE administrators were not dubious about these developments, for many of the same reasons as their teachers. A realization of the seeming lack of alternatives, however, led some within the ECE administration to work energetically to derive the greatest possible benefits from these events. As one ECE administrator said, in impatient reference to the reluctant Parent-nursery teachers: "The elementary school seems to be the future of early childhood programs. Rather than mourning the loss of their little empires, those teachers should be figuring out how to make the most out of the system."

The question of the extent to which early childhood educators will be able to maintain their professional "integrity" in their new organizational setting of public schools is, of course, a crucial one—one demanding an empirical study in its own right. But whatever the outcome of that struggle, it is undeniable that in some respects, the early educators' goal of "professionalization" will be advanced by movement into this new organizational base. Among other implications, the movement into the schools carries the potential to upgrade the personnel working in early childhood programs and to put them on a significantly higher salary scale than those working in non-public school settings.[16]

To summarize this discussion of the accommodations made by ECE, we have seen that by presenting itself as committed to a "cognitive" program, the organization managed at once to strengthen the loyalties of its black clients and to further entrench early childhood programs within

16. A very rough idea of the comparative advantage of public settings for early childhood educators comes from the 1970 Census. The median earnings for female pre-kindergarten and kindergarten teachers in 1970 in public institutions was $3,042; for their counterparts in private schools, it was $1,890. These figures are not entirely satisfactory for our purposes because they include kindergarten as well as pre-kindergarten teachers, and the figures also do not reflect the part-time employment that is more characteristic of private settings. Also, the "public" designation refers to situations other than public schools, such as Head Start programs. Nonetheless, the figures do suggest the relative advantages, to early childhood educators, of public-sector employment. The 1970 Census also showed that publicly based early educators had completed a median of 16.4 school years, in comparison with 14.4 years completed by teachers in private institutions. U.S. Bureau of the Census, "Summary of Social and Economic Characteristics of Prekindergarten and Kindergarten Teachers, 1970."

the BUSD. But though the development of this more "academic" identity serves important rhetorical functions, it also creates some practical problems—problems that are most directly experienced by the classroom staff. The issue of how to actually implement the new curriculum—and, indeed, the more fundamental question of what *is* an appropriate "cognitive curriculum" for three- and four-year-olds —remain dramatically unresolved. To conclude, a more "cognitive" self-presentation clearly brings more legitimacy to early childhood programs within the BUSD, but at a price. In the final chapter, I will consider again some of the likely costs of success.

7

The Prospects of Childcare: The Ascendancy of the Educators

This study has been shaped by two separate, yet related, concerns: the efforts of early childhood educators to transform themselves from "weak" professionals into more "powerful" ones; and the competing claims of a number of groups to define and control childcare services. In this final chapter, I intend to link these two themes more directly. First, I will analyze some of the processes by which early childhood education seems to be achieving a more "professionalized" status. Then, returning to the unresolved issues of national childcare policy which were raised in Chapter One, I will consider the implications of an increasing tendency toward educationally defined childcare, delivered through public schools.

THE PROFESSIONALIZATION OF EARLY CHILDHOOD EDUCATION

The movement upward of a professionalizing group typically involves a number of processes. In analyzing early childhood education, I will not offer an exhaustive list of all the contingencies facing emergent professions. Rather, I will suggest that five problems—and their apparently successful resolution by leaders within early childhood education—are particularly useful in explaining the current ascendancy of the profession. These problems concern its clientele, the body of knowledge it claims, the re-education of its practitioners, competition with neighboring occupations, and securing an organizational base.

Securing the Commitment of an Adequate Clientele

One defining characteristic of well-established professions, such as medicine and law, is a stable understanding of the relationship between professional and client. For professions such as early childhood education, which are both marginal and upwardly mobile, understandings about clients are in a state of flux. Many questions—such as the composition of the client population, the exact services to be offered by the profession, and the behaviors that are expected from clients —remain to be answered.

As with many other professions, the designation of a client population has not been entirely in the hands of early educators themselves. Because of the way the profession has historically been organized—into private nursery schools—the clientele has been drawn largely from the middle and upper classes. Events of the 1960s, most notably the Head Start program, brought a huge new population within the range of early childhood educators. In tracing the history of Berkeley's Parent-nurseries, I have shown that with the passage of California preschool legislation in 1965, the original middle-class group was joined by an influx of low-income, largely black clients. My argument is that each of these client groups is "valuable" to the profession in its own way. Each group, however, has somewhat different definitions of the services it wants from the profession. Thus one major problem facing early educators has been to maintain the commitments of its old constituency while successfully accommodating itself to the wishes of the new group.

What is it that the profession wants from clients? In the broadest terms, early educators want their clients to mobilize themselves as a *childcare constituency*—that is, both to use childcare facilities regularly and to lobby continually before legislators, funding agencies, and the general public for support of preschool enterprises. Both the particular history of ECE and the general history of early childhood education programs reveal the usefulness and relative political strength of such a constituency.[1]

1. The political possibilities of a childcare "constituency" on a national level were especially apparent in the spring of 1973, when HEW suddenly announced severe cuts in

Though all clients, both "old" and "new," are expected to act similarly as childcare advocates, each group seems suited to perform specialized functions. The new clients, by virtue of having been labeled "culturally deprived," provide early childhood education with a strong link to the burgeoning compensatory education establishment. By claiming to serve this population, early childhood educators gain access to vastly increased resources, including special funding; they are also welcomed into larger organizational settings, notably the public schools, and within certain circles they receive a form of legitimacy that was lacking when the profession catered only to the children of the middle and upper classes. In essence, with the acquisition of this new clientele, the profession has moved toward the stature of a "social service."

In spite of the boost provided by a new clientele, leaders are also concerned to retain the commitments of the older client group. One reason is the greater resources to which this client group has access. Such resources mean, for example, that early childhood education programs can count on at least some paying clients. Another reason is the desire that the profession not become over-identified with compensatory efforts. Ample, vocal participation of "respectable" clients who want publicly provided childcare will, presumably, help make early childhood education's case for the universal appeal and relevance of their programs.

By arguing for the commitments of both new and old client groups, early childhood educators are essentially walking a tightrope. They are, on the one hand, claiming to be a legitimate—if not crucial—part of the compensatory education movement; at the same time, they are placing themselves at a distance from it, saying that their programs are designed for a universal audience. Conceivably, these various claims can be

federal support of various social services. For childcare programs, the implications were to be reductions in the number of programs, changes in the services to be provided in publicly funded childcare, and changes in the eligibility requirements of such programs. Childcare parents and professionals were among the leaders in a sustained period of public outcry, with mass demonstrations, letter-writing campaigns and the like, which led HEW to revise some of its original cuts. See *Federal Register,* "Service Programs for Families and Children and for Aged, Blind or Disabled Individuals," February 16, 1973; *Voice for Children,* "Council Responds to Country's Sense of Crisis over Regulations," March 1973, p. 1; "Senate Hearings on SRS Regulations," June-July 1973, p. 1; "Surprise Death for SRS Regulations," January 1974, p. 1; and Joel Havemann, "Impasse over Social Services Regulations Appears Broken," *National Journal Reports,* December 7, 1974, pp. 1840-1844.

juggled successfully, but the danger remains—and it is certainly recognized by ECE administrators—that in some situations early childhood education will be increasingly absorbed by, and identified with, the larger compensatory education establishment.

In order to secure client loyalties, the profession has had to make some concessions. The major concession to the new clientele is a changeover to a more cognitively oriented program. As our look at Parent-nursery classrooms suggested, this changeover has not occurred without resistance from the older clients. I have mentioned some of the devices used by ECE personnel to soften this resistance.

A second demand made on early childhood educators, by new and old clients alike, is for increased "daycare"—that is, for an increased number of hours of care for the children. This demand has not been effectively resolved. While the new clients strongly identify with the "educational" component of early childhood education (and the older clients can live with it), both are becoming frustrated with the traditional nursery format of a three-hour-per-day program. While some parents within each client group might not want to admit favoring "daycare" (because of its historically negative connotations), they are clearly eager for a longer program—perhaps a full day—that would include both "enrichment" and "custodial" functions.

In Berkeley, there is evidence of a gradual accommodation to such pressures. A variety of factors, including recent difficulties in recruiting a sufficient number of black families who are interested in the Parent-nurseries, has led the district to concentrate on a newer program model, the Early Learning Center. These centers, which accommodate children from the age of three through eight, have as their primary characteristic the fusion of "educational" and "daycare" objectives in the same facility.

Creation and Co-optation of a Body of Knowledge

All would-be professions must base their claims to authority and expertise on a body of knowledge and doctrine. As Wilensky points out, the optimal knowledge base is one that is neither too broad or "familiar sounding" nor—at the other extreme—too narrow and precise.[2] Historically, the technical base claimed by early educators has suffered from the former problem: the notion of supervised group care for young children—in spite of the educators' rhetoric about a program of "social

2. Harold Wilensky, "The Professionalization of Everyone?" p. 149.

and emotional enrichment''—simply sounded too much like glorified babysitting for the public to see such services as the realm of bona fide "professionals."

Another problem the educators have had in developing an adequate knowledge base goes back to the confusion about the primary client of the profession—is it the child or the parent? Not really understanding precisely for whom their professional skills are being mobilized, early educators have understandably had trouble in articulating a convincing basis for practice. While officially claiming the socio-emotional needs of the child as the rationale for their programs, they have been unable to ignore the immense attraction of the custodial aspect of their services, and in this sense the parents have been the "real"—if somewhat unacknowledged—clients.

Recent efforts by early childhood educators have been oriented both toward strengthening the intellectual underpinnings of their programs for children and, at the same time, toward constructing an ideological justification for supplementing the parental role. To accomplish the first task, the profession has turned increasingly to the work of Jean Piaget and other social scientists who have studied children from a developmental perspective. (This turn to the work of Piaget and others dovetails nicely, of course, with some clients' demands for a cognitive program.) As already noted, the net effect of this body of research is to focus attention on hitherto-ignored facets of children's learning capacities. Not only does such research indicate that children below the age of six can learn more than had been assumed, it further suggests that there is a crucial relationship between the early years of life and later intellectual development. In short, one can draw out of this body of research a justification for programs intended to nurture the cognitive abilities of young children—and this, of course, is precisely what early childhood educators are doing. Such a mandate for intellectually stimulating preschool programs is further intensified as the profession becomes more closely identified with a "culturally deprived" population. The argument then becomes that while such programs are greatly beneficial to all children, they are especially appropriate for children from "deficient" environments.

At the same time this knowledge base vis-á-vis children is being developed, some within early childhood circles are seeing the benefits of an ideological alliance with the women's movement.[3] Early

3. See, for example, *Voice for Children*, "Council Joins Forces with Women's Political Caucus," January 1973, p. 3. One of the first demands of the revived feminist

educators are finding it useful to take the side of the women's movement on several arguments: that parents (especially mothers) should not be burdened with total responsibility for their children; that women should not feel guilty for wanting free time for work or other pursuits; that, in effect, parents and children both benefit from periods of time spent away from one another. The logical outcome of such arguments—the establishment of a vast new network of childcare facilities—is, of course, potentially to the great advantage of early childhood educators. The arguments of the profession, in the context of women's liberation, can be summed up as follows: childcare is a right of both parent and child; the best kind of childcare programs are educational ones, run by early childhood educators. As the educational director of a California residential program for teenage mothers exulted at a meeting: "Let's face it—we're women's lib in action! Just because young women bear children doesn't mean they have to be mothers *all the time*. Our job is to help them with mothering, and to make it possible for them to do other things as well."

This relationship with women's liberation, which appears to be occurring somewhat unevenly throughout the profession, is not without its difficulties. If the movement's rationale for childcare is the "freeing" of the parent, then in some instances the profession might have some difficulties in carrying out a mandate, from other quarters, that required parent involvement.[4] Moreover, as the relationship between women's liberation and early childhood education grows more involved, it is possible that the former will raise issues that the latter will find hard to resolve. These might include allegations of "sexism"—of individual staff members, in the curricular materials, and within the structure of the profession itself. Some persons within the profession may be inclined to deal with such charges, and some may not. A study of this scope cannot, of course, adequately assess the relationship that the profession is developing with the women's movement, nor the stress

---

movement in the late 1960s was free childcare services, to be available on a twenty-four-hour basis. Elizabeth Hagen, "Child Care and Women's Liberation." A resolution at the most recent (October 1975) NOW Conference stipulated that "NOW have as one of its top four priorities the promotion of quality feminist childcare available to all who wish, regardless of their economic resources." NOW National Conference, "Program Resolutions," Philadelphia, October 24-27, 1975, p. 11.

4. To be sure, we must distinguish between required parent involvement and the "community control" which is strongly advocated in most feminist statements on childcare. The latter refers to the *right* to intervene, while the former suggests an *obligation* to participate. In practice, however, such a distinction is often difficult to draw.

that this alliance may be causing for some educators. My point is to show that in this evolving relationship, we again see how the structural situation of weakness and marginality in the profession creates a compulsion to seek potentially useful alliances. But these alliances come to take on lives of their own, and the new allies themselves seek to modify the character of the profession.

Re-Socialization of Personnel

As leaders of an occupational group try to remake their work into a "profession," they also try to upgrade their staff into "professionals." This process can bring on a period of great strain in the career of an emergent profession. Conflicts between "old-timers" and "the new breed" intensify as some of the former group resist the new conception of "professionalism." In ECE, the re-socialization of staff members is occurring around the two issues of "identity" and classroom practice. As for identity, it will be recalled that the original director mounted an early campaign to have qualified ECE staff placed on the district's regular salary scale; such a move, she believed, would help the staff think of themselves as teachers, not custodians. Similarly, staff members were encouraged to join teachers' unions and local early childhood professional associations as a means of strengthening their identification as educators. In the area of classroom practice, a redirection of effort is coming about because of pressures from clients and others to change the traditional model of the nursery "program." For early childhood administrators, this implies developing new policies of cognitive instruction, weaning staff members from old ways and teaching them new ones, and in some cases weeding out individuals who are unwilling or unable to make the necessary changes.

Such a re-education process naturally meets obstacles. For some nursery school teachers, particularly older ones, the adoption of "academic" goals violates the core of their professional training. Perhaps ironically, it is those staff members with the *most* professional training—albeit training of the "wrong kind"—who find it most difficult to switch from a socio-emotional focus to a more rigorous cognitive one. Teachers with less extensive training—those who began their careers as aides for example—are often less troubled by new goals for the simple reason that they did not formerly receive a strong indoctrination against them.

Even assuming staff willingness to change, however, early education leaders have to devise ways of making this new Piaget-oriented body of knowledge comprehensible and meaningful. Actual principles of classroom application have to be plucked out of what is universally acknowledged to be a highly abstract and difficult literature. These problems are further compounded in those situations, such as Berkeley's Parentnurseries, where there are widely divergent educational backgrounds among staff members.

Competition with Neighboring Occupations

Another problem faced by all newly professionalizing groups, but one that seems particularly true of human-relations occupations, is competition with neighboring occupations. Historically, the major professional rivalry within the field of preschool services has been that of early childhood education and social work. The rivalry is still very much alive, of course, and childcare systems are currently operated by each, but early childhood education appears to be gradually emerging as the leading force. Let us look briefly at some of the strategies by which it is edging out its main competitor, social welfare.

A main reason for the educators' ascendancy is that they have more successfully distanced themselves from the pathology associated with their rivals' brand of childcare. While social welfare-sponsored daycare has historically been oriented toward "casework" with the poor (and especially the "unfit" poor), nursery education's original purpose was to supply "enrichment" to middle-class children. Though early childhood education's clientele now includes large numbers of "deprived" children, and though some of its programs are now much more explicitly "compensatory" than before, still the profession remains in a better position than social welfare to make a case for the universal applicability of its services.

Another important element in early childhood education's emerging dominance is, quite simply, its successful assimilation of some of the practices of its rival. We have seen in the case of ECE that pressures at the state level compelled the organization to provide its clients with many of the social services typically provided by welfare workers. More importantly, on an informal level, the actual needs of ECE clients produced an "underground" response from the Parent-nurseries, so that a constant stream of social services began passing between staff and clients and between clients themselves. More generally, I have shown that the clients of ECE, while they might repudiate the stigma associated with "daycare," actually do prefer an extended period of care to the three-hour program traditionally associated with nursery schools. ECE's response to this has been to check the growth of its Parent-nurseries and concentrate its resources instead on programs which provide longer periods of care.

Securing an Organizational Base

One historic problem of early childhood education has been its failure to find an adequate organizational base in which to practice. The dominant organizational form—the private nursery school—has in several ways impeded a fuller development of the profession. Such private schools are, first of all, typically controlled by an active parent board; the professional staff, in a very immediate sense, serves at the pleasure of its clients. Another drawback of the private nursery is that it constrains early educators from attracting a great many potential clients; the traditional three-hour-per-day program, usually with high fees, means that "nursery schools" have largely been inaccessible to children of working and poor parents.[5]

This lack of an adequate organizational base also accounts for early childhood education's inability to regulate the entrance of new members into the profession. In addition to the private nursery, persons with early childhood education backgrounds find employment in a wide range of settings—public and private daycare centers, Head Start programs, and so forth—each of which has different requirements of staff training. Still others who identify as "early childhood educators" work in family daycare homes and unlicensed facilities of various kinds. Besides working in a variety of settings, they operate with a variety of degrees and credentials. There is no agreement yet on what constitutes the main entry-level degree for early childhood practitioners: currently, teachers enter classrooms with degrees ranging from a Master's degree received in a university setting to a "performance-based credential" which requires no formal schooling;[6] some facilities, including licensed ones, have no credential requirements whatsoever.[7]

5. In Berkeley in 1973, for example, typical fees for a private nursery school (three hours per day, five days per week) averaged around $40 per month. Fees are higher in schools without parent participation.

6. This "performance-based credential" refers to the Child Development Associate plan, a government-initiated proposal for a new category of early childhood personnel. "Individuals will be credentialed as Child Development Associates based on a demon-

The entrances of early childhood programs into public school systems—which is occurring in California and which is a likely possibility elsewhere—would to some degree solve most of these problems. The job security of early childhood personnel would no longer be directly tied to their clients. The number of children who could take part in early childhood programs would expand greatly. A higher degree of regulation of new members would become possible, with the opportunity to standardize required training and certification. The resources of modern school systems—higher salary scales and more benefits, special support services, the use of buses—would now become available. But beyond the influx of immense material benefits, absorption of early childhood programs into the public schools would seem to mark an important status passage in the career of early childhood education. It would imply a new legitimacy for this profession, which has always been marginal to public education.

CHILDCARE POLICY AND THE PUBLIC SCHOOLS

What if the trend, exemplified by Berkeley's ECE, of placing early childhood programs in the public schools were to continue? In particular, what will happen if the American Federation of Teachers and other allied groups[8] became successful in their demands that schools become "prime sponsors" of new federally supported childcare services? To examine the implications of a national childcare program that would be educationally defined and administered through local school systems,

---

strated competency rather than on completion of courses or acquisition of credit hours . . . certification will be based on an assessment of the individual's performance as an educator of young children, not upon our typical trappings of academic accomplishment." Edward Zigler, "A New Child Care Profession: The Child Development Associate."

At this writing, the CDA program remains at the experimental stage. Were the program to expand significantly, however, it could have implications for early childhood education's "professional" aspirations by loosening the training requirements of staff in various federally funded programs. See also CDA Consortium, "The CDA Consortium at a Glance;" and Ray Williams, "CDA-'75."

7. Office of Child Development, *Abstracts of State Day Care Licensing Requirements.* See also Sally Allen, "Early Childhood Programs in the States."

8. Other groups which have either endorsed or come close to the AFT position include: the American Association of School Administrators, Council of Chief State School Officers, National Congress of Parents and Teachers, the National Education Association, the National School Boards Association, and the Executive Council of the AFL-CIO. See *Day Care and Child Development Reports,* February 16, 1976, pp. 3-4.

let us return to the major issues of childcare policy that were raised in Chapter One.

In discussing the development of a national childcare policy, I indicated that the following were especially problematic: the actual purpose of childcare programs, the population for which they are intended, the form and content of the programs, the anticipated role of parents, and the administration and control of the programs. Childcare delivered through the schools, we can speculate, would resolve these issues in the following directions: the manifest purpose of the programs would be the "enrichment" of young children; the target population would be a universal one (though not necessarily free to all participants), offered on a voluntary basis;[9] the format would be a mixture of half and whole "school day" programs, that is, three- and six-hour programs, and some longer ones; the content of the programs would be "comprehensive," that is, a mixture of educational and health components, as well as a custodial one; parent participation would probably not be required, though, in most instances, it would be strongly encouraged, on a rhetorical level at least; the administration of programs would be in the hands of local school districts, whether the early childhood programs were located on "regular" school sites or in separate facilities.

Clearly, the greatest advantage that public school auspices would bring is the promise of a destigmatization of publicly funded childcare. If offered through the schools, and made universally accessible, public childcare programs would no longer be socioeconomically segregated, nor confined to "special" populations, such as welfare or "problem" families. Another obvious advantage of educational control is that programs can be expected to have some "educational" content and not merely be custodial operations. Also, compared with many presently operating childcare facilities, public school auspices would imply higher and uniform standards in such matters as teacher-child ratios, adequacy of physical facilities, and the health of participating children and adults.

These advantages notwithstanding, certain issues remain problematic with the prospect of school-controlled childcare. The most basic of

9. AFT position papers on universal childcare and virtually all other current proposals would make such programs voluntary. One might speculate, however, that if childcare were to be located in the schools, and began to generate "average daily attendance" revenues, that there would ultimately be pressures to lower the age of compulsory school attendance.

these is how effectively such arrangements will meet the needs of working parents. Most existing early education programs, both within the public schools and elsewhere, typically run for only three hours per day; even if they were extended to a full school "day," that would imply a program running only from 9 A.M. to 3 P.M. Thus, for parents holding an average full-time job, three or four hours of care before and after school is essential. Were the schools to gain prime sponsorship of new childcare programming, a crucial question becomes the extent to which school officials would be receptive to fusing "daycare" concerns with "educational" ones.

However, even if the schools did become more flexible in this respect—following the lead of California's Children's Centers, for example, which operate from early morning until early evening—some families will still be left without necessary services. One obvious example would be parents, especially single ones, who work night or weekend shifts. Some parents, moreover, apparently prefer non-institutional settings for childcare, such as "family daycare" homes. The family daycare home is presently the arrangement used by the overwhelming majority of daycare users; even if other choices were expanded, home-based childcare would quite likely remain the preferred choice of many of the present users, especially the parents of infants and toddlers. Although statements from the AFT acknowledge that not all childcare under school *sponsorship* necessarily has to be located on public school *sites,* it may be questioned how receptive various school systems would be to the use of alternative sites, especially if they had gained control of childcare funding. It is this need for a variety of programs to meet the needs of diverse familites that leads some within early childhood circles to oppose the exclusive control of childcare by the schools. Even while acknowledging an important role for school-delivered programs, they fear that exclusive control would preclude funding and other support for alternative models, especially home-based ones.

The extent to which parents would be welcome participants in school-delivered childcare is also unclear. The Parent-nursery situation in Berkeley suggests that while some contemporary parents feel oppressed by an obligation to participate, vitually all of them find it very important to have the right to do so. Some school districts, such as the BUSD, seem to have a genuine commitment to parent involvement in the classroom, even above the preschool level. Others do not. While the AFT claims that school-delivered childcare "can bring parents closer to the schools," skeptics point to the union's general record of hostility toward community involvement, and in particular to its lack of interest in involving families in childcare services.[10] It is, of course, difficult to predict how parent participation might evolve in different situations of school-administered childcare. It does seem probable, however, that in many instances schools will not sustain the tradition of intense parent involvement that has been a staple of other preschool situations, especially the nursery school.

The issue of appropriate staff training for early childhood programs within the schools is also problematic. Given the present haphazard and often minimal staff requirements for many childcare programs, it is undeniably true, as the AFT argues, that public school control will bring an upgrading of childcare personnel. But what the AFT means by "upgrading" refers rather narrowly to a certain number of years of education and a "regular" teaching credential. One result of this kind of "upgrading" will almost certainly be that experienced early childhood personnel will find their positions jeopardized by more "qualified" teachers with no early childhood background whatsoever. For example, as the events within Berkeley unfold, it appears that with the total number of budgeted teaching positions being frozen, teachers with elementary teaching credentials are able to force out those holding a less-powerful credential, such as the Children's Center "permit" held by many junior members of the Parent-nursery staff. In a similar vein, the control of early childhood education staffing policies by school bureaucrats will make the difficult issue of "community control" over staffing positions even more complex, particularly by thwarting the wishes of low-income clients to be incorporated into staff ranks.

These predictable tensions over parent involvement and staff qualifications might be seen as symptoms of a more fundamental incompatibility between early childhood education and its possible new host, the public schools. As indicated in the last chapter, the public schools are in a position to sabotage some unique features of nursery-school programs.

---

10. One of the AFT's strongest critics, particularly on the point of family involvement, has been Theodore Taylor, Executive Director of the Day Care and Child Development Council of America. "Mr. Shanker advocates dropping 'family' from the title of the Child and Family Services Act because he believes 'that a bill to provide children's services, and especially early childhood education, should not be called a "Family Services Bill" nor attempt to provide such services.' *We can never compromise on that.*" Theodore Taylor, "Child Care in the Schools: A Position Paper," p. 14. See also Joseph Michalek, "Tug of War: Who'll Get Preschool Children?" *New York Times*, January 15, 1975, p. 73.

The argument over a "socio-emotional" curriculum versus an "academic" one that already rages within the profession will doubtlessly become greatly intensified in public school sites, with the "academic" forces having the advantage. Most importantly, perhaps, the delicate compromise that can be made in the autonomous Parent-nursery sites—"learning through creative play"—will be difficult to sustain as the programs move to elementary school locations. As one ECE supervisor said bitterly, when contemplating the move to public schools: "They don't want us coming in there, bringing all our sand and water with us." In short, movement into the elementary schools implies a devaluation of play, the cornerstone of nursery-school practice and theory, and will exert strong pressures on the nursery to adopt an elementary school regimen: larger classes, smaller adult-to-child ratios, fixed recess periods, and finally—what is most disturbing to traditionalists—an inordinate administrative interest in providing evidence of academic instruction.

Early Childhood Education in the Schools: The Pitfalls of Success

My argument throughout this book has been that the ability of early childhood education to gain a foothold in the public schools would represent an important move upward for this "weak" profession. Similarly, in the case of ECE, I suggested that the incorporation of its programs directly into elementary schools would bring a new stability to early childhood programs within the BUSD. But as I have just explained, this new setting will extract significant compromises from early childhood education. To some degree, the problems and tensions arise simply because of the different nature of the two educational enterprises: elementary schools are typically larger in size, organized along different lines, and set up to accomplish different objectives than nursery schools. But the troubles that early childhood programs are experiencing, as they settle into their new base, reflect another fact: *the larger system they have joined is itself in crisis.* Public schools in general—and Berkeley's are no exception—are currently experiencing a certain breakdown in public confidence. (It is this very atmosphere of crisis, I have argued, that contributes to the district's current interest in ECE.) In Berkeley, where the schools have served as a national model of integration, the crisis centers specifically around the persistent gap in achievement between white and non-white children. Thus, in order to understand the full implications of ECE's incorporation into "regular schools," we must also take note of the ways in which early childhood programs and teachers are affected by the generalized atmosphere of crisis and accountability in the district.

One effect of the larger crisis on ECE can be seen in the pedagogical techniques that are being endorsed by central BUSD administrators. The promotion of "behavioral modification" is a prime example. The alleged success of behavioral modification programs when applied to minority children[11] has led to enthusiasm for the philosophy on the part of key administrators, particularly those charged with elementary education. In the past few years, elementary teachers including ECE personnel, have been taken to behavioral modification workshops in Los Angeles, been shown films, and in a variety of other ways have been exhorted to adopt this particular orientation. While the reactions of ECE staff members vary, some of them find the principles of behaviorism especially repugnant. Behaviorism is seen as the very antithesis of the classic nursery model of relating to children. (As Naomi, a Parent-nursery "old-timer" said, after viewing a film demonstrating behavioral techniques in a preschool classroom, "I want to tell a child I like him even if he gets the answer wrong!") On a formal level, of course, no teacher is compelled to adopt behavioral techniques (or any others). On an informal level, however, in a situation of mounting job insecurity, ECE administrators and teachers alike feel increasing pressures to please "the administration;" for this reason, a certain drift toward behaviorism in ECE classrooms seems inevitable.

Testing is another issue that impinges on ECE because of the larger crisis within the Berkeley schools. Some testing has always taken place within ECE programs, in order to fulfill state requirements. But entrance into the public schools—at a time of strain—greatly intensifies the amount of testing, and the attention given to it.

Testing, like behaviorism, is seen by some Parent-nursery staff members as a blatant affront to nursery school philosophy. Sarah indignantly asked: "How can you 'test' how a child feels about himself? How can you 'test' his well-being?" Yet offensive as testing may be to some, it also represents one of the most likely avenues of ECE mobility within the district. It is through testing that the organization can "prove" it is "working"—that it is, in fact, raising the achievement levels of minority children.

As in so many other instances, ECE personnel are here caught in a contradictory situation. Testing is objected to on both moral and

---

11. John and Helen Krumboltz, *Changing Children's Behavior.*

educational grounds, yet its political potential cannot be denied. Ironically, therefore, a chronic complaint among some within ECE is that the organization is never given adequate resources to do "a really thorough job of testing."

Finally, the most striking indication that ECE has entered a crisis-ridden system lies in the heavy pressure for public accountability that faces the BUSD. For the past few years, California public school teachers have been regulated by the Stull Bill, a piece of legislation that calls for routine teacher evaluation against a set of stated objectives.[12] The intent behind this measure is to identify and weed out teachers who are not reaching their district's goals.

Many schoolteachers, including those in Berkeley, are, predictably, upset by the Stull Bill. In order to mollify teachers' fears, many school districts have delegated to teachers themselves the major responsibility for specifying the objectives on which they are to be evaluated. Nevertheless, the Stull Bill presents a curious problem for ECE staff members, because they have had great difficulty generating behavioral and educational objectives. The "cognitive"-"social" split over curriculum and the current dissension over pedagogical techniques make it almost impossible for staff members to agree on criteria for external evaluation. As in the testing debates, this situation is made worse by what some staff members perceive as the impossibility of measuring nursery-school goals. One teacher said: "My primary objective with three-year-olds is the child's acceptance of himself—how are they going to know if I achieved that?"

This particular emergency situation generated by the Stull Bill reveals a more general dilemma facing the organization. The implementation of the Bill, which requires a specification of program goals, comes dangerously close to suggesting that at present ECE has no rationalized "program," in the manner of elementary or secondary schools. Crises like this one are thus particularly distressing to the organization because they indicate the present incompatibility of traditional nursery education and the demands of modern school districts.

Similar pressures for accountability come from within the district itself. During the course of this study, an ad hoc parents' group, Black Parents for Education, demanded of the school board that the district inform parents of the expectations of pupil achievement at each grade

12. California A.B. 293.

level.[13] Precise expectations of children in early childhood education and kindergarten programs were also included in the demands of this parent group.

As with the Stull Bill, this demand was quite upsetting for ECE teachers, for they themselves have no shared conception of what "each child is supposed to know" by the time he or she finishes an ECE program and enters kindergarten. Most likely, the classic nursery-school teacher's response to such a question would be that "the child should know what he is capable of knowing." Such an answer, of course, is highly unsatisfactory to those who posed the initial question, and thus ECE is further pressured toward rationalizing its curriculum.

The issues of behaviorism, testing, and public accountability illustrate the types of pressures being exerted on early childhood education as it is gradually absorbed by public education. This new organizational base will doubtless be of great importance for the future growth and stability of early childhood education. Yet, as we have seen, this growth has its price. The prospect of school-administered childcare raises disturbing questions for both early childhood educators and their clients. From the educators' perspective, the question is whether school bureaucracies will allow them the space to retain the essentials of a nursery program.[14] For parents, the question is whether childcare located directly within the schools will allow for the same program flexibility, informality, and accessibility that characterized smaller, decentralized facilities, such as ECE's Parent-nurseries. It is too soon to tell how these issues will be resolved in the Berkeley context. As school-controlled and school-delivered childcare is debated on a na-

13. Black Parents for Education, "Concerns for Education in Berkeley," mimeo, February 20, 1973.

14. One early childhood educator, in response to the threat faced by the profession, has called for "undercover" work in the schools: "In a school world obsessed with reading scores, with grades, with IQ divorced from life functioning . . . can anyone care about a child's needs to make his own meaning? In a school world that forces teachers to 'cover' a fixed amount of material in a fixed time span, that grades teachers on the order and quiet of their classrooms, ... that severely limits teachers' freedom to respond to needs of the moment—can one listen to a child's unique views and personal feelings? Here and there are teachers who skillfully and courageously resist the pressures for conformity, the package approach to learning, the preference for procedure over process that have become endemic in our country. And it *takes* skill and courage—because the powers of repression are strong, in education as well as in politics. It also takes careful analysis of the power patterns in a school so one can intelligently plan the strategies for child-based curriculum, when, and whom to resist, when not to, how far to go, what [should be] the important first step." Dorothy Gross, "Encouraging the Curious Mind: Through the Curriculum," p. 5.

tional level, it is these issues—as well as those of cost and feasibility —that I belive should be considered by policy makers, educators, and parents.

CHILDCARE INSTITUTIONS
AND FAMILY LIFE

To conclude, let us return to the issue with which this book began: the relationship between childcare and the family. Regardless of one's political perspective, the prospect of a national system of childcare —whether school-controlled or not—raises disturbing questions. Some argue that universal childcare would "destroy" the family. While I do not think that any childcare system in itself would be capable of destroying the family, certainly programs that were compulsory and closed to parental involvement would in many ways be damaging to family integrity. (At the same time, certain models of childcare pose a threat to emergent family forms precisely because they *do* involve parents. A prime example of the newly fashionable programs of home-based early education, which are built around the instruction of mothers of young children; such programs not only impose a set of childrearing techniques, they also promote an ideology which stipulates that "good" mothers stay at home.)[15] The public schools, as the potential administrative arm of new programs, also leave uncertain the question of childcare and family relations: a look at the schools' undistinguished record of "outreach" to parents makes one wary of the prospect of very young children entering such unresponsive bureaucracies.

Real as these dangers are, I believe it would be equally dangerous to blind ourselves to the promise contained in the idea of universal childcare. Although these phrases may now sound like empty rhetoric, it is worth repeating that childcare really could be an important step in the "liberation" of mothers, both working and non-working,[16] simi-

15. One of the most prominent and ambitious new programs, the Brookline Early Education Project, appears to be oriented, both practically and philosophically, only toward non-working mothers. See Maya Pines, "Head Head Start;" and Burton White, "Reassessing Our Educational Priorities."

16. Certainly childcare would also benefit fathers. I put the stress on mothers because at present they are generally the ones most directly responsible for children. This is especially true in single-parent families. In 1974, there were 4,580,000 single-parent families headed by women and only 519,000, headed by men. Ross and Sawhill, *Time of Transition,* p. 12.

larly, there is every reason to believe that childcare really could "enrich" children, and that high-quality programs might properly be seen as the "right" of all young children, irrespective of their parents' circumstances. There is another conceivable benefit of childcare — one that has been largely overlooked even by its advocates. This is the paradox that *childcare itself opens up new possibilities of family life.* The potential of childcare in this sense becomes clear if we shift our conception of "family life" from *home*-based activities to *experiences* that strengthen bonds between family members. By making itself accessible, in non-coercive ways, to family members other than the preschoolers themselves, the childcare center can become a highly useful setting for interaction between family members.

The idea that a childcare program should absorb as many family members as possible and promote interaction between them is already present to a limited extent in some ECE programs, such as the Parent-nurseries. But ECE leaders are eager to develop the idea further, especially in centers which serve working parents and have little formal parent participation. When asked about their hopes for future programs, the family motif was a particularly strong one. The director of the model new Early Learning Center in Berkeley visualizes the Center becoming a multi-purpose community institution, ideally one that serves clients from "womb to tomb." "I'd like to have laundry machines put in the Center. I'd like people whose kids are here to do their laundry here and spend time with us then. . . . I'd like to have breakfast programs for the parents, even those that work, and discuss nutrition with them." Two other administrators, who supervise all-day programs for children of working parents, talk of serving family-style dinners to parents and children at the end of the working day. "After a hard day's work, these parents complain that they are too tired to go home and put a dinner on the table. That's what we should be doing for them." A fourth ECE supervisor has developed a proposal for a "Sibling Center," at which older brothers and sisters of the child actually enrolled in ECE programs could also become involved.

One could argue, of course, that such plans merely reflect the desires of aspiring professionals for an ever-widening clientele and range of programs. Also, the notion of family units spending large blocs of time under institutional auspices inevitably raises issues of social control. While I would not deny the professional ambitions of early educators nor the possibilities of social control inherent in a mass childcare system, I think the above-mentioned proposals indicate that the ECE leadership is aware of the fact that family life as it is commonly mythologized in American culture does not exist for many of its clients. It is a myth, and no more. The diversity of ECE families is mirrored in the larger society: on a national level, the number of single parents heading households, the labor force participation of both single and married mothers, and the number of absent-from-home parents maintaining some contact with their children all contribute to the difficulty of maintaining the home as the predominant arena of family life. This does not mean, of course, that persons in "irregular" situations, or even traditional couples, who from an ideological standpoint are reexamining their assumptions about parenthood, no longer value the emotions associated with "family life;" it does mean that, increasingly, such persons are relying on selected institutions[17] to help supply experiences that previously had taken place at home.[18]

Historically, American social services have been very intolerant of non-conventional forms of family life. I will hazard no firm prediction that the future will be different. I would stress, however, that a client-responsive, universally available childcare system holds out at least the promise of a genuine acceptance of diverse family arrangements; and, in a period in which the health of the family as an institution is being questioned daily, it could promote rewarding exchanges between family members. In light of the bad press that American childcare has received throughout its history, it is ironic that its imminent role perhaps is not to erode family life further, but to help salvage it.

17. Residential homes for single parents and their children are another contemporary instance of service institutions which facilitate "family life" among relatives. See Evelyn Benas, "Residential Care of the Child-Mother and Her Infant: An Extended Family Concept;" and Florence Kreech, "A Residence for Mothers and Their Babies."

18. In a sense, this notion of out-of-home family life suggests a reversion to older historical forms of the family, in which the distinction between "public" and "private" life was not so pronounced. See Eli Zaretsky, *Capitalism, The Family, and Personal Life.*

Postscript

After this study was completed, two events occurred within the Berkeley Unified School District that have relevance to the issues raised in this book. The first is that ECE was dismantled as a separate unit within the district; its five-woman administration was disbanded, and the various programs that had been under ECE jurisdiction, as well as Compensatory Education and Special Education (handicapped) programs, now came under one newly created administrative post, the Director of Early Childhood and Elementary Curriculum. The second is that the Berkeley School Board increased the Children's Center Override Tax, and in so doing generated additional income to expand Children's Center places and staff positions.

Each of these events, on one level, might be taken to represent a further stabilization of early childhood programs within the BUSD. The administrative reorganization suggests that early childhood concerns are now on a par with elementary ones; the increase in Children's Center places indicates an increasing legitimacy of this program, which has historically been scorned as a "babysitting" operation.

Yet, at the same time, these developments further reveal the uncomfortable fit between the needs of early childhood programs and the needs of public school systems. Placing preschool programs within a large administrative unit that has responsibility for a variety of other programs will probably threaten the preservation of a unique "early childhood" identity for programs formerly within ECE. The increase in the number of Children's Center places was conceived primarily as a *fiscal* measure, rather than as a commitment to the Centers. The raising of the Override Tax was virtually the only way the school board could generate income without going to the voters for new taxing authority. The newly created staff positions at the Centers were filled not with persons with specialized early childhood training, but largely with BUSD teachers from a variety of backgrounds, presently without

152

classroom assignments, to whom the District was compelled to offer some classroom arrangement.

These events hardly tell the whole story of how early childhood programs are faring within the BUSD. As I have already indicated, I believe it is too soon to make policy inferences from the Berkeley situation. I would suggest that the organizational and fiscal imperatives that these events typify must be considered in any discussion of school-delivered childcare.

Bibliography

Abbott, Grace. *The Child and the State*. Vols. I and II. Chicago: University of Chicago Press, 1938.

Abt Associates. *A Study in Child Care*. Vol. IIB: *Systems Case Studies*. Cambridge, Mass., 1971.

— — —. *A Study in Child Care*. Vol. III: *Cost and Quality Issues for Operators*. Cambridge, Mass., 1971.

Adams, Paul, et al. *Children's Rights: Toward the Liberation of the Child*. N.Y.: Praeger, 1971.

Allen, Salley. "Early Childhood Programs in the States." *Child Care—Who Cares?* Edited by Pamela Roby. N.Y.: Basic Books, 1973, pp. 191-227.

Almy, Millie. "Spontaneous Play: An Avenue for Intellectual Development." *Young Children* (May 1967): 268-277.

— — —. "Piaget in Action." *Young Children* 31, No. 2 (January 1976): 93-96.

American Federation of Teachers. *Early Childhood Education: A National Program*. Washington, D.C., December 1974.

American Teacher, Vol. 59, March 1975. Special magazine supplement on Early Childhood Education.

Anderson, Robert, and Harold G. Shane. *As the Twig Is Bent: Readings in Early Childhood Education*. N.Y.: Houghton Mifflin Co., 1971.

Architectural Research Laboratory. *An Annotated Bibliography on Early Childhood*. University of Michigan, 1970.

Aries, Philippe. *Centuries of Childhood: A Social History of Family Life*. N.Y.: Vintage, 1962.

Auleta, Michael, ed. *Foundations of Early Childhood Education: Readings*. N.Y.: Random House, 1969.

Bane, Mary Jo. "Open Education." *Harvard Educational Review* 42, No. 2 (May 1972): 273-281.

Baratz, Stephen S., and Joan C. Baratz. "Early Childhood Intervention: The Social Science Base of Institutional Racism." *As the Twig Is Bent*. Edited by Robert Anderson and Harold G. Shane. Boston: Houghton Mifflin, 1971, pp. 34-52.

Barbrack, Christopher, and Della Horton. "Educational Intervention in the Home and Paraprofessional Career Development: A First Generation Mother

Study.'' *Darcee Reports,* Vol. 4, No. 3, George Peabody College for Teachers, Nashville, Tenn., 1970.

———. "Educational Intervention in the Home and Paraprofessional Career Development: A Second Generation Mother Study with Emphasis on Costs and Benefits.'' *Darcee Reports,* Vol. 4, No. 4, George Peabody College for Teachers, Nashville, Tenn., 1971.

Barker, Linda. "Preprimary Enrollment: October 1972.'' National Center for Educational Statistics, U.S. Department of Health, Education, and Welfare, Public No. (OE) 73-11411.

Beck, Helen. "Pressure in the Nursery.'' *Children Today* (Sept.-Oct. 1972): 26.

Becker, Howard. "The Culture of a Deviant Group: The Dance Musician.'' *The Outsiders.* N.Y.: Free Press, 1963.

———. "The Nature of a Profession.'' In *Sociological Work,* pp. 87-103. Edited by Howard Becker. Chicago: Aldine, 1970.

———. "The Teacher in the Authority System of the Public School.'' In *Sociological Work,* pp. 151-164. Edited by Howard Becker. Chicago: Aldine, 1970.

———, ed. *Sociological Work.* Chicago: Aldine, 1970.

Becker, Howard, et al. *Institutions and the Person: Papers Presented to Everett C. Hughes.* Chicago: Aldine, 1968.

Beer, Ethel. *Working Mothers and the Day Nursery.* N.Y.: Whiteside, Inc., 1957.

Benas, Evelyn. "Residential Care of the Child-Mother and Her Infant: An Extended Family Concept.'' *Child Welfare* 54, No. 4 (April 1975): 290-294.

Bergstrom, Joan M., and Gwen Morgan. "Issues in the Design of a Delivery System for Day Care and Child Development Services to Children and Their Families.'' The Day Care and Child Development Council of America, Inc., Washington, D.C., 1975.

Berkeley Unified School District. "Buildings in Berkeley.'' Report of Harold Maves, Assistant Superintendent, March 1973.

———. "Early Childhood Education Programs,'' 1972.

———. *The Early Learning Center: A New School for Instruction and Day Care for Children 3-8 years,* Spring 1970.

———. "Fact Sheet on Alternatives,'' January 1974.

———. "Report of Staff Racial Census,'' Office of Research and Evaluation, October 1973.

———. "School Master Plan Report,'' October 1967.

Bernard, Jessie. *Women and the Public Interest.* Chicago: Aldine, 1971.

Bettelheim, Bruno. *The Children of the Dream: Communal Childrearing and American Education.* N.Y.: Avon, 1969.

Bissell, Joan. "The Cognitive Effect of Pre-School Programs for Disadvantaged Children.'' Ph.D. thesis, Harvard University, 1970.

Black Child Development Institue. "From a Black Perspective: Optimum Conditions for Minority Involvement in Quality Child-Development Programming." In *Child Care—Who Cares?* pp. 71-85. Edited by Pamela Roby. N.Y.: Basic Books, 1973.

Black Parents for Education. "Concerns on Education in Berkeley." Document presented to BUSD, 20 February 1973. (Mimeographed.)

Bloom, Benjamin. *Stability and Change in Human Characteristics.* N.Y.: John Wiley, 1964.

Bourne, Patricia Gerald. *Daycare Nightmare: A Child-Centered View of Child Care.* Berkeley: University of California, working paper 145 of the Institute of Urban and Regional Development, 1971.

— — —. "The Three Faces of Day Care." In *The Future of the Family,* pp. 268-281. Edited by Louise K. Howe. N.Y.: Simon and Schuster, 1972.

— — —. "The Unconglomerated Agglomerate: Child Care and the Public Sector." Ph.D. thesis, University of California, Berkeley, 1974.

Bowles, Samuel. "Education and Socialist Man in Cuba." In *Schooling in a Corporate Society,* pp. 272-303. Edited by Martin Carnoy. N.Y.: David McKay, 1972.

Braun, Samuel J., and Esther P. Edwards. *History and Theory of Early Childhood Education.* Worthington, Ohio: Charles A. Jones, 1973.

Bremer, Robert H. *Children and Youth in America: A Documentary History, Vol. II: 1866-1932.* Cambridge: Harvard University Press, 1971.

Bronfenbrenner, Urie. *Two Worlds of Childhood.* N.Y.: Russell Sage Foundation, 1970.

Bruner, Jerome. "The Course of Cognitive Growth." *American Psychologist* 1 (1964): 1-15.

— — —. *Toward a Theory of Instruction.* Cambridge: Belknap, 1967.

Bucher, Rue, and Anselm Strauss. "Professions in Process." *American Journal of Sociology* 66 (January 1961): 325-334.

Butler, Annie. "Early Childhood Education: A Perspective on Basics." *Childhood Education* 50 (October 1973): 21-25.

California State Department of Education. "The Early Childhood Education Program Proposal," Sacramento, 1972.

— — —. "Report of Task Force on Early Childhood Education to Superintendent Riles," Sacramento, 1971.

Caldwell, Bettye M. "On Designing Supplementary Environments for Early Child Development." In *As The Twig Is Bent: Readings in Early Childhood Education,* pp. 233-244. Edited by Robert Anderson and Harold G. Shane. Boston: Houghton Mifflin, 1971.

— — —. "Infant Day Care—The Outcast Gains Respectability." In *Child Care-Who Cares?* pp. 20-36. Edited by Pamela Roby. N.Y.: Basic Books.

— — —. "A Timid Giant Grows Bolder," *Saturday Review,* February 21, 1971, pp. 47-66.

Caliguri, Joseph. "Will Parents Take Over Headstart Programs?" *Urban Education* (April 1970): 53-64.

Carr-Saunders, A. M., "Metropolitan Conditions and Traditional Professional Relationships." In *The Metropolis in Modern Life*, pp. 279-288. Edited by R. M. Fisher. Garden City: Doubleday, 1955.

Carr-Saunders, A. M., and P. A. Wilson. *The Professions*. Oxford: Clarendon Press, 1933.

Chapman, Judith, and Joyce Lazar. Interagency Panel on Early Childhood Research and Development, "A Review of the Present Status and Future Needs in Daycare Research," Washington, D.C., November 1971.

Clark, Burton R. *Adult Education in Transition: A Study of Institutional Insecurity*. Berkeley: University of California Press, 1968.

– – –. "Organizational Adaptation and Precarious Values." *American Sociological Review* 21 (1956): 327-336.

Clinchy, Evans. "The Boardman Elementary School." In *Radical School Reform*, pp. 297-306. Edited by Ronald and Beatrice Gross. N.Y.: Simon and Schuster, 1969.

Cohen, Dorothy. "This Day's Child in School." *Childhood Education* 51 (October 1974): 8-15.

Cook, Ann, and Herbert Mack. "Business in Education: The Discovery Center Hustle." *Social Policy* (Sept.-Oct. 1970): 5-11.

Cremin, Lawrence. The Transformation of the School. N.Y.: Random House, 1961.

Davis, Mary D., and Rowena Hansen. *Nursery Schools: Their Development and Current Practices in the United States*. Office of Education Bulletin No. 9. Washington, D.C.: Government Printing Office, 1932.

Davis, Mary D. *Schools for Children under Six*. U.S. Office of Education Bulletin 15, 1947. Washington, D.C.: Government Printing Office, [1947].

Day Care and Child Development Council of America, Inc. "Bulletin: HEW's Revisions on May 1 Regulations," Washington, D.C., September 28, 1973.

– – –. *The Care and Education of Young Children*. Washington, D.C., 1972.

– – –. "Standards and Costs for Day Care," Washington, D.C., 1968.

– – –. "Toward Comprehensive Child Care," Day Care Consultation Service, Washington, D.C., 1975.

Denzin, Norman K. *Children and Their Caretakers*. New Brunswick, N.J.: Transaction, 1973.

Dill, John. "The Black Child and Child-Care Issues." In *Child Care-Who Cares?*, pp. 273-283. Edited by Pamela Roby. N.Y.: Basic Books, 1973.

Dowley, Edith. "Perspectives on Early Childhood Education." In *As The Twig Is Bent*, pp. 12-21. Edited by Robert Anderson and Harold G. Shane. Boston: Houghton Mifflin, 1971.

Dratch, Howard. "The Politics of Child Care in the 1940s." *Science and Society* 38 (Summer 1974): 167-204.

Durkheim, Emile. *Education and Sociology*. Glencoe, Ill.: Free Press, 1956.

Ehrenreich, Barbara, and John Ehrenreich. "Health Care and Social Control" *Social Policy* (May-June 1974).

Eliot, Abigail Adams. "Nursery Schools Fifty Years Ago." *Young Children* (April 1972): 209-214.

Ellis, Katherine, and Rosalind Petchesky. "Children of the Corporate Dream: An Analysis of Day Care as a Political Issue under Capitalism." *Socialist Revolution*, No. 12 (November-December 1972): 9-28.

Emergency Nursery Schools During the First Year (1933-1934). Report of the National Advisory Committee on Emergency Nursery Schools. Washington, D.C.: Government Printing Office [1935].

Emlen, Arthur C. "Slogans, Slots, and Slander: The Myth of Day Care Need." *American Journal of Orthopsychiatry* 43, No. 1 (January 1973): 23-45.

Erlanger, Howard. "Social Class and Corporal Punishment in Childrearing: A Reassessment." *American Sociological Review* 39 (February 1974): 68-85.

Evans, Ellis. *Contemporary Influences in Early Childhood Education*. N.Y.: Holt, Rinehart and Winston, 1971.

Executive Office of the President: Office of Management and Budget. *Social Indicators, 1973*, "Prekindergarten Enrollment." Washington, D.C.: U.S. Government Printing Office, 1973.

Featherstone, Joseph. "Kentucky Fried Children," *The New Republic*, September 12, 1970, pp. 12-16.

Fein, Greta, and Alison Clarke-Stewart. *Day Care in Context*. N.Y.: John Wiley, 1973.

Fisher, Bernice. "Claims and Credibility: A Discussion of Occupational Identity and the Agent-Client Relationship." *Social Problems* (Spring 1969): 423-32.

Forbes, "Corporate Baby-sitting," June 1, 1971, pp. 19-20.

Foster, Josephine, and Marion L. Mattson. *Nursery School Education*. New York: D. Appleton-Century Co., 1939.

Frank, Lawrence. "The Fundamental Needs of the Child." *Mental Hygiene* 22 (July 1938): 353-379.

Freidson, Eliot. "The Impurity of Professional Authority." In *Institutions and the Person*, pp. 25-34. Edited by Howard Becker et al. Chicago: Aldine, 1968.

– – –. "The Organization of Medical Practice." In *Handbook of Medical Sociology*, pp. 299-319. Edited by Howard Freeman et al. Englewood Cliffs, N.J.; Prentice-Hall, 1963.

– – –. *Patients' View of Medical Care*. N.Y.: Russell Sage, 1961.

– – –. *Profession of Medicine*. N.Y.: Dodd, Mead and Co., 1970.

– – –. *Professional Dominance: The Social Structure of Medical Care*. N.Y.: Atherton, 1970.

Freudenthal, Daniel K. "Evolution of School Desegregation in Berkeley, California." In *Man the Measure: The Crossroads,* pp. 31-49. Edited by D. Adelson. N.Y.: Behavioral Publications, 1972.

Frost, Joe L., and Thomas G. Rowland. *Curricula for the Seventies.* Boston: Houghton Mifflin, 1969.

Frost, Joe L. *Early Childhood Education Rediscovered.* N.Y.: Holt, Rinehart and Winston, Inc., 1968.

Furstenberg, Frank. *Unplanned Parenthood: The Social Consequences of Teen-aged Childbearing.* N.Y.: Free Press, 1976.

Gans, Herbert J. *The Urban Villagers: Group and Class in the Life of Italian-Americans.* N.Y.: Free Press, 1962.

Gartner, Alan, and Frank Reissman. *The Service Society and the Consumer Vanguard.* N.Y.: Harper & Row, 1974.

Geer, Blanche. "Occupational Commitment and Teaching." In *Institutions and the Person,* pp. 221-234. Edited by Howard Becker et al. Chicago: Aldine, 1968.

Goffman, Erving. *Encounters: Two Studies in the Sociology of Interaction.* Indianapolis: Bobbs-Merrill, 1961.

— — —. *The Presentation of Self in Everyday Life.* N.Y.: Doubleday, 1959.

Goldner, Fred, et al. "Priests and Laity: A Profession in Transition." *The Monographs of the Sociological Review* 20 (1973).

Goldstein, Joseph, Anna Freud, and Albert J. Solnit. *Beyond the Best Interests of the Child.* N.Y.: Free Press, 1973.

Goode, William J. "Encroachment, Charlantanism, and the Emerging Professions: Psychology, Medicine and Sociology." *American Sociological Review* 25 (1960): 902-914.

Gordon, Ira J. *Parent Involvement in Compensatory Education.* Urbana: University of Illinois, 1968.

— — —. *Reaching the Child Through Parent Education: The Florida Approach.* Gainesville: University of Florida, 1969.

Graubard, Allen. *Free the Children: Radical Reform and the Free School Movement* N.Y.: Pantheon, 1972.

Gray, Susan W. "Home Visiting Programs for Parents of Young Children," *Darcee Reports,* Vol. 5, No. 4, George Peabody College for Teachers, Nashville, Tenn., 1971.

Greenberg, Polly. *The Devil Has Slippery Shoes: A Biased Biography of the Child Development Group of Mississippi.* Toronto: Macmillan, 1969.

Greenwood, Ernest. "Attributes of a Profession." *Social Work* 2 (July 1957): 44-55.

Gross, Dorothy. "Encouraging the Curious Mind: Through the Curriculum." *Childhood Education* 51 (Oct. 1974): 5-7.

Grotberg, Edith, ed. *Day Care: Resources for Decisions*. Washington, D.C.: Office of Economic Opportunity, 1971.

Hagen, Elizabeth. "Child Care and Women's Liberation." In *Child Care—Who Cares?*, pp. 284-298. Edited by Pamela Roby. N.Y.: Basic Books, 1973.

Hammerman, Ann, and Susan Morse. "Open Teaching: Piaget in the Classroom." *Young Children* (Oct. 1972): 41-54.

Harvard Educational Review. "Special Issues on Children's Rights," Vol. 43, No. 4 (November 1973).

Haug, Marie R., and Marvin B. Sussman. "Professional Autonomy and the Revolt of the Client." *Social Problems* 17, No. 2 (Fall 1969): 153-160.

Head Start Child Development Programs. *A Manual of Policies and Instructions*. Washington, D.C.: Office of Economic Opportunity, 1971.

Hellmuth, Jerome, ed. *Disadvantaged Child*. N.Y.: Brunner Mazel, 1970.

Henton, Emma. "The Nursery School Movement in England and America." *Childhood Education* 1 (May 1925): 413-417.

Hess, Robert, et al. "Parent Involvement in Early Education." In *Day Care: Resources for Decisions*, pp. 265-298. Edited by E. Grotberg. Office of Economic Opportunity, 1971.

— — —. "Parent-Training Programs and Community Involvement in Day Care." In *Day Care: Resources for Decisions*, pp. 199-312. Edited by E. Grotberg. Office of Economic Opportunity, 1971.

Highberger, Ruth, and Sharon Teets. "Early Schooling: Why Not? A Reply to Raymond and Dennis Moore." *Young Children* 29, No. 2 (Jan. 1974): 66-78.

Hirsch, Elizabeth S. "Accountability: A Danger to Humanistic Education." *Young Children* 31, No. 1 (Nov. 1975): 57-66.

Hoenig, Alice S. "Curriculum for Infants in Day Care." *Child Welfare* 53 (Dec. 1974): 633-642.

Hughes, Everett C. *Men and Their Work*. Toronto: Free Press, 1958.

— — —. "The Professions in Society." *The Canadian Journal of Economics and Political Science* 26, No. 1 (February 1960): 54-61.

— — —. The Sociological Eye: *Selected Papers on Work, Self, and the Study of Society*. Vol. II. Chicago: Aldine, 1971.

Human Events. "Nixon Must Veto Child Control Law," October 9,1971, p. 1.

Hunt, J. McVicker. *Intelligence and Experience*. N.Y.: Russell Sage, 1961.

— — —. *Human Intelligence*. New Brunswick, N.J.: Transaction Books, 1972.

Johnson, Harriet M. *Children in the Nursery School*. N.Y.: John Day, 1928.

Joffe, Carole. "Child Care: Destroying the Family or Strengthening It?" In *The Future of the Family*, pp. 261-267. Edited by Louise K. Howe. N.Y.: Simon and Schuster, 1972.

Kahn, Alfred, and Mayer, Anna. "Day Care as a Social Instrument: A Policy Paper." N.Y.: Columbia University School of Social Work, 1965.

Katz, E., and B. Danet. *Bureaucracy and the Public: A Reader in Official Client Relations.* N.Y.: Basic Books, 1973.

Katz, Michael, ed. *School Reform: Past and Present.* Boston: Little, Brown, 1971.

Katz, Sanford. *When Parents Fail: The Law's Response to Family Breakdown.* Boston: Beacon Press, 1971.

Kerr, Virginia. "One Step Forward—Two Steps Back: Child Care's Long American History." In *Child Care-Who Cares?,* pp. 157-171. Edited by Pamela Roby. N.Y.: Basic Books, 1973.

Keyserling, Mary Dublin. *Windows on Day Care.* N.Y.: National Council of Jewish Women, 1972.

Klein, Jenny. "Symposium: CDA—The Child Development Associate." *Childhood Education* (March 1973).

Kohn, Melvin L. *Class and Conformity: A Study in Values.* Homewood, Ill.: Dorsey, 1969.

———. "Social Class and Parental Values." *American Journal of Sociology* 64 (January 1959): 337-351.

Kreech, Florence. "A Residence for Mothers and Their Babies." *Child Welfare* 54, No. 8 (Sept.-Oct. 1975): 581-592.

Kraft, Ivor. "Head Start to What?" *The Nation,* September 5, 1966, pp. 179-183.

Krumboltz, John, and Helen Krumboltz. *Changing Children's Behavior.* Englewood Cliffs, N.J.: Prentice-Hall, 1972.

Ladner, Joyce. *Tomorrow's Tomorrow: The Black Woman.* N.Y.: Anchor, 1972.

Lally, J. Ronald, and Lucille Smith. "Family Style Education: A New Concept for Preschool Classrooms Combining Multi-age Grouping with Freedom of Movement among Classrooms." Paper presented at Meeting of American Psychological Association, September 1970.

Lally, J. Ronald, et al. "Training Paraprofessionals for Work with Infants and Toddlers." *Young Children* (Feb. 1973): 173-181.

Landreth, Catherine. *Education of the Young Child.* N.Y.: John Wiley and Sons, 1942.

Lazerson, Marvin. "The Historical Antecedents of Early Childhood Education." In *Early Childhood Education: The Seventy-first Yearbook of the National Society for the Study of Education, Part II.* Chicago: University of Chicago Press, 1972.

———. *Origins of the Urban School: Public Education in Massachusetts.* Cambridge: Harvard University Press, 1971.

———. "Social Reform and Early Childhood Education: Some Historical Perspectives." In *As The Twig Is Bent,* pp. 22-33. Edited by Robert Anderson and Harold G. Shane. Boston: Houghton, Mifflin, 1971.

Leff, Mark H. "Consensus for Reform: The Mothers'-Pension Movement in the Progressive Era." *Social Service Review* 47 (Sept. 1973): 397-417.

Lefton, Mark, and William R. Rosengren, eds. *Organizations and Clients: Essays in the Sociology of Service.* Columbus, Ohio: Charles Merrill, Inc., 1968.

－－－. "Organizations and Clients: Lateral and Longitudinal Dimensions." *American Sociological Review* 31 (December 1966): 802-810.

Lewis, Elizabeth. "The Real California Report: A New Approach to Education." *Phi Delta Kappan* 54 (April 1973): 558-561.

Lewis, Mary R. "Day Care under the Social Security Act." *Social Service Review* 48 (September 1974): 428-437.

Lichtenberg, Philip, and Dolores G. Norton. *Cognitive and Mental Development in the First Five Years.* Chevy Chase, Md.: National Institute of Mental Health, 1970.

Lortie, Dan. "The Partial Professionalization of Elementary Teaching." In *The Semi-Professions and Their Organization,* pp. 15-30. Edited by Amitai Etzioni, N.Y.: Free Press, 1969.

Low, Seth, and Pearl Spindler. *Child Care Arrangements of Working Mothers in the United States,* HEW, Children's Bureau Publication No. 461, 1968.

Marshall, T. H. *Class, Citizenship and Social Development.* New York: Anchor, 1965.

－－－. "The Recent History of Professionalism in Relation to Social Structure and Social Policy." *Canadian Journal of Economics and Political Science* (August 1939): 325-340.

Mayer, Rochelle. "A Comparative Analysis of Preschool Curriculum Models." In *As The Twig Is Bent: Readings in Early Childhood Education,* pp. 286-314. Edited by Robert Anderson and Harold G. Shane. Boston: Houghton Mifflin, 1971.

Mead, Margaret. *The School in American Culture.* Cambridge: Harvard University Press, 1951.

Merton, Robert, and Elinor Barber. "Sociological Ambivalence." In *Sociological Theory: Values and Sociocultural Change,* pp. 91-120. Edited by Edward Tiryakian. N.Y.: Free Press, 1963.

Miller, Donald. "Governing Childcare Centers: Basic Considerations." In *Child Care-Who Cares?,* pp. 86-97. Edited by Pamela Roby. N.Y.: Basic Books, 1973.

Moore, Evelyn K. "It's Happening . . . in Childcare." *Black Child Advocate* (June 1972): 2.

Moore, Raymond S., Robert D. Moon and Dennis R. Moore. "The California Report: Early Schooling for All?" *Phi Delta Kappan* 53 (June 1972): 615-621.

Moore, Raymond S. "Further Comments on the California Report." *Phi Delta Kappan* 53 (April 1973): 560-561.

National Society for the Study of Education. Twenty-Eighth Yearbook. "Preschool and Parental Education," Bloomington, Illinois, 1929.

– – –. Forty-Sixth Yearbook, Part II. "Early Childhood Education." Chicago: University of Chicago Press, 1948.

– – –. Seventy-First Yearbook, Part II. "Early Childhood Education." Chicago: University of Chicago Press, 1972.

Nixon, Richard. "Veto Message—Economic Opportunity Amendments of 1971," December 10, 1971, 92nd Congress, 1st Session, Document No. 92-48.

Office of Child Development. *Abstracts of State Day Care Licensing Requirements*. Washington, D.C.: Government Printing Office, 1971.

Omwake, Eveline B. "The Child's Estate." In *Modern Perspectives in Child Development*, pp. 277-294. Edited by Albert Solnit and Sally Provence. N.Y.: International Universities Press, 1963.

Owen, Grace. *Nursery School Education*. N.Y.: E. P. Dutton and Co., 1920.

Perot, Ruth Turner. "Daycare and the Black Community: Myths and Realities," Detroit, Merrill-Palmer Institute, 1971 Lecture Series.

Perrow, Charles. *Complex Organizations: A Critical Essay*. Glenview, Ill.: Scott, Foresman and Co., 1972.

Pines, Maya. "Head Head Start," *New York Times* Magazine, October 26, 1975.

– – –. *Revolution in Learning*. N.Y.: Harper and Row, 1966.

Read, Katherine H. *The Nursery School*. Philadelphia: W. B. Saunders, 1955.

Riles, Wilson. "The First Eight Years." *The American Teacher* 59 (May 1975): 6-8.

Roby, Pamela, ed. *Child Care-Who Cares? Foreign and Domestic Infant and Early Childhood Development Policies*. N.Y.: Basic Books, 1973.

Ross, Heather L., and Isabel V. Sawhill. *Time of Transition: The Growth of Families Headed by Women*. Washington, D.C.: The Urban Institute, 1975.

Roth, Julius, Sheryl Ruzek, and Arlene K. Daniels. "Current State of the Sociology of Occupations." *The Sociological Quarterly* 14 (Summer 1973): 309-333.

Rothman, Sheila. "Other People's Children: The Day Care Experience in America." *The Public Interest* 30 (Winter 1973): 11-27.

Rowe, Mary Potter, and Ralph D. Husby. "Economics of Child Care: Costs, Needs, and Issues." In *Child Care-Who Cares?*, pp. 98-122. Edited by Pamela Roby. N.Y.: Basic Books, 1973.

Ruderman, Florence. *Child Care and Working Mothers: A Study of Arrangements Made for Daytime Care of Children*. N.Y.: Child Welfare League of America, 1965.

Sale, June S. "Family Day Care: One Alternative in the Delivery of Developmental Services in Early Childhood." *American Journal of Orthopsychiatry* 43, No. 1 (January 1973): 37-45.

– – –. "Watch: Family Day Care Mothers Work Together To Improve Services." *Children Today* 4 (Sept.-Oct. 1975): 22-24, 36.

Sandberg, John H., and Pohlman, Joanne D. "Reading on the Child's Terms." *Young Children* 31, No. 2 (January 1976): 106-112.

Schorr, Alvin. *Children and Decent People*. N.Y.: Basic Books, 1974.

Schultz, David. *Coming Up Black*. Englewood Cliffs: Prentice-Hall, 1969.

Schwartz, Charlotte Green. "Strategies and Tactics of Mothers of Mentally Retarded Children for Dealing with the Medical Care System." In *Diminished People, The Problems and Care of the Mentally Retarded*, pp. 73-195. Edited by Norman Bernstein. Boston: Little, Brown, 1970.

Scott, Robert A. "The Selection of Clients by Social Welfare Agencies: The Case of the Blind." *Social Problems* 14, No. 3 (Winter 1967): 248-257.

Seeley, John R., R. A. Sim, and E. W. Loosley. *Crestwood Heights: A Study of the Culture of Suburban Life*. N.Y.: John Wiley, 1963.

Selznick, Philip. *Leadership in Administration*. N.Y.: Harper and Row, 1957.

Shanker, Albert. "Early Childhood Education is a Job for the Public Schools," *New York Times,* September 9, 1974, p. 11.

– – –. Statement before the Senate Subcommittee on Children and Youth and the House Subcommittee on Special Education Programs on the Child and Family Services Act of 1975, June 5, 1975. Distributed by American Federation of Teachers, Washington, D.C.

Sibley, Carole. *Never a Dull Moment: The History of a School District Attempting To Meet the Challenge of Change*. Berkeley, California: Documentation and Evaluation of Experimental Projects in Schools, 1972.

Slater, Philip. "Social Change and the Democratic Family." In *The Temporary Society*, pp. 20-52. Edited by Warren Bennis and Philip Slater. N.Y.: Harper and Row, 1968.

Spock, Benjamin. "How Not To Bring Up a Bratty Child," *Redbook,* Feb. 1974, pp. 29-31.

Stearns, Miriam. "Report on Pre-School Programs: The Effect of Pre-School Programs on Disadvantaged Children and Their Families." Report submitted to the Office of Child Development, 1971.

Steiner, Gilbert. *The State of Welfare*. Washington, D.C.: The Brookings Institution, 1971.

Steinfels, Margaret O'Brien. *Who's Minding the Children? The History and Politics of Day Care in America*. N.Y.: Simon and Schuster, 1973.

Strauss, Anselm, et al. "The Hospital and Its Negotiated Order." In *The Hospital in Modern Society*, pp. 147-169. Edited by E. Freidson. N.Y.: Free Press, 1963.

– – –. *Psychiatric Ideologies and Institutions*. N.Y.: Free Press, 1964.

Taylor, Theodore. "Child Care in the Schools: A Position Paper," Day Care and Child Development Council of America, Inc., Washington, D.C., 1975.

Trey, J. E. "Women in the War Economy." *Review of Radical Political Economics* 4, No. 3 (July 1972): 41-57.

U.S. Bureau of the Census. "Enrollment in Public and Private Schools: 1960 to 1973." *Statistical Abstract of the United States, 1974*. Washington, D.C., 1974.

– – –. *Occupational Characteristics*, PC (2), 7A, 1970.

U.S. Department of Health, Education, and Welfare. *Digest of Educational Statistics*. U.S. Government Printing Office, 1975.

U.S. Department of Labor, Women's Bureau. *Facts about Women Heads of Households and Heads of Families*. Washington, D.C., 1973.

U.S. Office of Economic Opportunity. *Day Care Survey: 1970*. Westinghouse Learning Corporation and Westat Research, Inc., 1971.

U.S. Senate, Committee on Finance. *Child Care Data and Materials*. Washington, D.C.: Prentice Hall, 1966.

Vollmer, Howard, and Donald L. Mills. *Professionalization*. Englewood Cliffs, N.J.: Prentice Hall, 1966.

Vygotsky, Lev. *Thought and Language*. Cambridge: MIT Press, 1962.

Waldman, Elizabeth. "Children of Working Mothers, 1974." *Monthly Labor Review 98* (January 1975): 64-67.

Wall Street Journal. "Growing Pains: Day Care Franchises, Beset with Problems, Find Allure Is Fading," November 27, 1972, p. 1.

Waller, Willard. *The Sociology of Teaching*. N.Y.: John Wiley, 1967. (Originally published in 1932.)

Walsh, James Leo, and Ray Elling. "Professionalism and the Poor." *Journal of Health and Social Behavior* 9 (1968): 16-28.

Ware, Carolyn. *Greenwich Village: 1920-1930*. Boston: Houghton Mifflin, 1935.

Weber, Evelyn; "The Function of Early Childhood Education," *Young Children*, June 1973, pp. 265-274.

– – –. *Early Childhood Education: Perspectives on Change*. Worthington, Ohio: Chas. A. James, 1970.

– – –. *The Kindergarten: Its Encounter with Educational Thought in America*. N.Y.: Teachers College Press, 1969.

Weiss, Robert S. "Helping Relationships: Relationships of Clients with Physicians, Social Workers, Priests and Others." *Social Problems* (Winter 1973): 219-328.

Westinghouse Learning Corporation. *The Impact of Project Head Start: An Evaluation of the Effects of Head Start on Children's Cognitive and Affective Development*. Athens, Ohio: Ohio University, 1969.

Wheelwright, E. C., and Bruce McFarlane. *The Chinese Road to Socialism*. N.Y.: Monthly Review Press, 1970.

White, Burton. *The First Three Years of Life*. Englewood Cliffs, N.J.: Prentice-Hall, 1975.

– – –. "Reassessing Our Educational Priorities." Paper presented to Education Commission of the States Early Childhood Education Symposium, Boston, August 1974.

White, Burton, et al. "When Should Schooling Begin?" *Phi Delta Kappan* 53 (June 1972): 610-614.

Wilensky, Harold. "The Professionalization of Everyone?" *American Journal of Sociology* 70, No. 2 (September 1964): 138-156.

Williams, Ray. "CDA-'75." *Childhood Education* 51 (March 1975): 267-272.

Wilkerson, Albert K. *The Rights of Children: Emergent Concepts in Law and Society.* Philadelphia: Temple University Press, 1973.

Williams, C. Ray, and Thomas F. Ryan. "Competent Professionals for Quality Child Care and Early Education: The Goal of CDA," *Young Children,* December 1972, pp. 71-74.

Young, D.R., and R. R. Nelson, eds. *Public Policy for Day Care of Young Children.* Lexington, Mass.: D. C. Heath, 1973.

Zaretsky, Eli. *Capitalism, The Family, and Personal Life.* N.Y.: Harper and Row, 1976.

Zigler, Edward. "A New Child Care Profession: The Child Development Associate," *Young Children,* December 1971, pp. 71-81.

Index